ARCHDUKE FRANZ FERDINAND LIVES!

ARCHDUKE FRANZ FERDINAND LIVES!

A World Without World War I

Richard Ned Lebow

palgrave
macmillan

ARCHDUKE FRANZ FERDINAND LIVES!
Copyright © Richard Ned Lebow, 2014
All rights reserved.

First published in 2014 by PALGRAVE MACMILLAN® in the U.S.—a division of St. Martin's Press LLC, 175 Fifth Avenue, New York, NY 10010.

Where this book is distributed in the UK, Europe and the rest of the world, this is by Palgrave Macmillan, a division of Macmillan Publishers Limited, registered in England, company number 785998, of Houndmills, Basingstoke, Hampshire RG21 6XS.

Palgrave Macmillan is the global academic imprint of the above companies and has companies and representatives throughout the world.

Palgrave® and Macmillan® are registered trademarks in the United States, the United Kingdom, Europe and other countries.

ISBN: 978-1-137-27853-1

3 9082 12305 1347

Library of Congress Cataloging-in-Publication Data

Lebow, Richard Ned.
   Archduke Franz Ferdinand lives! : A world without World War I / Richard Ned Lebow.
       pages   cm
   Includes bibliographical references and index.
   1. World War, 1914–1918—Influence. 2. Imaginary histories. 3. World politics—1919–1932. I. Title.
   D523.L437   2013
   940.3'11—dc23

                                                                    2013014401

A catalogue record of the book is available from the British Library.

Design by Letra Libre, Inc.

First edition: January 2014

10 9 8 7 6 5 4 3 2 1

Printed in the United States of America.

To Greg Massell

*Who would have had a less stressful life and longer-lived
parents and brother in either counterfactual world*

Contents

1
Possible Worlds

IT IS AUGUST 2014, AND THE NORTHERN HEMISPHERE IS experiencing a second month of exceptionally lovely weather. Americans have just celebrated the one hundredth anniversary of the opening of the Panama Canal, hailed in retrospect, along with its sister Suez Canal, as transportation links that facilitated globalization and helped forge a century of peace. In Balmoral the aging but spry Queen Elizabeth II is hosting Prince Harry and his German bride, Princess Elizabetha. The princess's father, younger brother of the kaiser, named her after the British queen in recognition of the excellent relations between these two long-intermarried families of constitutional monarchs. In Jerusalem, under the authority of the Great Powers Condominium for the Holy Land, renewed clashes have occurred between Orthodox Jews and their Muslim counterparts at the Temple Mount. In India the governor general, Gurchuran Singh, is on holiday at a hill station but has met with representatives of India's sporting and business elite for a briefing on their preparations for hosting next year's Commonwealth Games. They will hold events in all of India's major cities, from Dacca in the east to Karachi in the west.

This fantasy world might have been our world if World War I had not been fought. For reasons I make clear in the book, many aspects of life would be better. Nearly a century of peace among the great powers would have made large military establishments and arms races things of the past, allowing vast sums of money to go to infrastructure, education, health care, urban renewal, and foreign aid. The standard of living would be higher and poverty all but nonexistent in the developed world, as it is in today's Scandinavia. Without either world war or the Holocaust, the Jewish population of Europe would be large and thriving, but Israel would not exist.

A downside is inevitable. Governments would have made massive investments in weapons and weapons-related developments. So penicillin, nuclear energy, radar and safe long-distance air travel, and the information revolution would have been delayed. So too would civil rights in the United States in the absence of the massive migrations of Negro workers to the war plants of the East, Midwest, and the Pacific coast during both world wars. Neither Barack Obama nor anyone else of African descent could have been elected president of the United States. Colonialism would have had a longer shelf life, although India, Israel-Palestine, and Cyprus would have avoided partition and the bloody conflicts that followed.

Why focus on World War I and its consequences? It wiped out a generation of young men and killed large numbers of civilians through disease, ethnic cleansing, and the civil wars that arose in its aftermath. The war hastened the ascendancy of the United States as the world's leading economic power; led to the breakup of the German, Austro-Hungarian, Russian, and Ottoman empires; and set in motion a chain of events that would ultimately lead to the end of the British, French, Spanish, and Portuguese empires as well. It triggered a revolution in Russia, which had repercussions in eastern and central Europe and more lasting resonance in China and Southeast Asia. Collectively these developments made it almost impossible to restore political and economic stability to Europe, thus paving the way for Hitler's rise to power, the Holocaust, and a second, far more deadly, bid for domination by Germany in alliance with Italy and Japan. World War II in turn gave rise to a cold war between the Soviet bloc and the West that kept Europe divided for fifty years, a target of thousands of nuclear weapons that—at the push of a button—could have left the continent a desolate, uninhabitable no-man's-land. World War I was, without question, the defining event of the twentieth century.

World War I and the events that followed had equally profound cultural and intellectual consequences. Europe's self-confidence was lost along with its leading role in the world, a psychological turn that was evident in the increasing defiance, doubt, confusion, and alienation of postwar art, literature, and music. Many artists and intellectuals sought refuge in a highly idealized image of Soviet-style socialism. Matters were, if anything, worse in the immediate aftermath of World War II. The United States became the leader of the self-proclaimed Free World. It financed the reconstruction of western Europe and Japan, imposed US political and economic institutions and practices wherever it could, and gained influence in a wider circle of states through aid, trade, and investment. Extraordinary levels of investment at home in education and research, charitable support for the arts, and emigration of thousands of Europe's leading scientists, artists, and intellectuals made the United States the world's leader in medicine, science, space exploration, and the creative arts. American popular culture became global in its appeal, leading some intellectuals to worry about Hollywood's takeover of culture and others to celebrate it as a "soft power" resource.

To fathom the consequences of World War I, we must know what our world might have been like without it. We cannot turn back the historical clock or access parallel universes to create or discover alternative worlds. Our only recourse is to engage in counterfactual thought experiments. My what-ifs cannot undo the devastation of World War I, but constructing possible fictional worlds can help bring to light some causes and consequences of the war. The imaginary worlds I describe are the most plausible best and worst worlds that might have arisen in the absence of World War I. Of course other scenarios might have emerged. This margin for error is not a problem because I am not suggesting that either world was the most likely to arise. Rather, they define the limits of the worlds that might have come about and thus the envelope in which any of them, including the most probable, would be found.

I use the terms "best" and "worst" worlds in an entirely relative sense. They are not the best or worst worlds that you or I can imagine, as the best world has a nasty downside and the worst world some good features. Rather, they are the best and worst worlds that might reasonably have evolved in the absence of World War I. The best world is far from being a utopia, although the worst world certainly qualifies as a dystopia. Are they "better" and "worse" worlds than the one in which we live? This is a matter of judgment, and readers will form their own opinions. The so-called "best" world is, I believe, a "better" world than ours. It avoids two World Wars, the Holocaust, the Russian Civil War, the Soviet Union and communism, and the deaths of almost 100 million people. There is a price: tolerance of all kinds is delayed, as are the scientific and engineering breakthroughs that lead to antibiotics, safe air travel, and computer and information technology. It seems a fair trade-off as these developments all ultimately occur and many more people survive to enjoy them.

Why would we imagine alternative lives? Because what-ifs are a useful, often necessary, means of evaluation. If you want to assess your choice of partner, school, job, or car—or even the book you are reading—you have two ways of going about it. One is to try an alternative. This is relatively easy to do with books, as you can put one down and pick up another. It can work with jobs if the economy is good. With automobiles you can rent a different model or take a spin in a friend's car. Unless your partner or spouse is unusually understanding, trying another one out for several months of comparison is more difficult. The same is true for universities, many jobs, and places of residence. Your only recourse may be to imagine what it would be like to have a different partner, school, job, home, city, or country. People do this every day. They spontaneously conduct counterfactual experiments to evaluate their lives or aspects of them.

Numerous studies suggest that people are most likely to resort to counterfactuals when they are unhappy about choices they have made. They invent "upward" counterfactuals that lead to better outcomes and make them feel better. This works best when people also convince themselves that they had little choice but to act as they did, thus minimizing their responsibility for negative outcomes. Alternatively people resort to "downward" counterfactuals that lead to worse outcomes and serve as wake-up calls to prompt preparatory responses.

I use both kinds of counterfactuals in this study. In the next chapter I do away with World War I and anything like it. Then I use an upward counterfactual to construct a better, more peaceful, world. I am not convinced, and neither should you be, that our world was in any way inevitable. I contend that World War I was a highly contingent event that could easily have been derailed. From the vantage point of 1914, that is, from the perspective of contemporary politicians, generals, and pundits, the war came as a surprise. Widespread expectations of continuing peace were by no means unreasonable. They may look this way from our perspective, but that is because we know the world went to war. In its aftermath politicians and generals wrote self-serving memoirs to advance the case for its inevitability.

I then invoke a downward counterfactual, on the grounds that avoiding war in 1914 would not necessarily have led to a better world. It could have produced a nastier and highly unstable one. This may be the harder case to make, given the extraordinary horrors of the twentieth century. Germany's defeat in World War I led to Hitler, World War II, the Holocaust, the political division of Europe, and fifty years of cold war. In Asia the Japanese invasion of China triggered another bloodbath, as did post-1945 wars of independence in the Dutch East Indies (now Indonesia), Malaya, Indochina, Madagascar, and Algeria. Asia and the Middle East saw a slew of postcolonial wars. What could possibly have been worse?

Imagine the survival of a conservative authoritarian Germany, a revolution in Russia, and an alliance of both countries and Japan. Then throw in successful development of atomic weapons by Germany and their use in a war against the Western democracies. Once again, the point of the exercise is not to make the case that this scenario, or any other I examine, would have come to pass, only that they were possible. What-ifs of this kind offer insights into the world in which we actually live. They let us probe why and how it came about, how contingent it was, and how we should evaluate it. They allow us to think more intelligently about the causes, contingency, and consequences of events that did occur, and this is my avowed goal.

And, lest you think that these grand historical sweeps are pure whimsy, I show how my alternative worlds would have affected real people. I create counterfactual biographies of the war's actors, victims, and others affected by it. All their lives would have played out quite differently in these different worlds. Some achieve fame for different reasons, and others live more ordinary lives. Some also live longer, as they do not die in World War I, the influenza epidemic, World War II, or the Holocaust.

My life, and that of my original family, offers a graphic illustration of how individual lives are affected by larger historical developments. To the best of my knowledge my parents fled to Paris in the hope of escaping the Nazis, and I was born there in 1941. In July 1942 the French National Police (Milice) rounded up the foreign Jewish population. I was saved by an ordinary French police officer (*flic*), to whom my mother handed me before being pushed into a freight car and shipped to Drancy and Auschwitz. This courageous and well-intentioned man later handed me over to a group of French Jewish women who had organized to protect children. I was subsequently hidden in a village, smuggled over the Pyrenees into Spain, and then shipped out of Lisbon to New York with one hundred other Jewish orphans. Immigration officials looked the other way, and we were offloaded at night and sent to orphanages.

I was adopted by an American Jewish family that provided the love and guidance all children need. One need not go any further to recognize how incredibly lucky I was in comparison to most other Jewish children born in Nazi-occupied Europe. My life could easily have ended in 1942. Also fortuitous was the goodwill of US immigration officials and my adoption by a wonderful couple. I was lucky again when my adoption became legal five years later, and the judge, having figured out that my papers were phony, had the court issue me a birth certificate with New York City as my place of birth.

My early life is more dramatic than most and would have been different in either alternative world. So would yours, although in ways different from mine. By thinking about what your life, and perhaps the lives of your parents, would have been like in the worlds I am about to create, you will develop a much better appreciation of how World War I and its consequences affected your life.

2

Preventing World War I

COUNTERFACTUAL MEANS CONTRARY TO FACTS. A COUN-
terfactual describes an event that did not occur. In everyday language
counterfactuals can be described as what-if statements. This nicely cap-
tures their purpose: they vary some feature of the past to change some
aspect of the present. Some people use counterfactuals to imagine different futures, although strictly speaking they pertain only to the past.
Counterfactuals make changes in the past (antecedents) and connect
them via a chain of events to a change in the present (consequent). I
contend that if Franz Ferdinand and Sophie had not been assassinated
(antecedent), then World War I could have been averted (consequent).

Historical counterfactuals always involve some degree of speculation because, as evolutionary biologist Stephen J. Gould laments, we
cannot rerun the tape of history to see what would actually happen
in the new circumstances that counterfactuals create. This is equally
true of so-called "factual" history. If we assert that Hitler was responsible for the Holocaust, we must consider what would have happened
in Germany if he had never become its dictator. Every historical claim

rests on a counterfactual, but these alternative worlds are rarely, if ever, examined.

The fictional nature of counterfactuals makes many scholars, especially historians, wary of them. Counterfactual experiments often make use of evidence as rich as that incorporated in any factual argument. Even when evidence is meager or absent, the difference between counterfactual and "factual" history is much less than commonly supposed. Documents rarely provide smoking guns that allow researchers to establish motives or causes beyond a reasonable doubt. Actors only occasionally leave evidence about their motives, and historians rarely accept such testimony at face value. More often, historians infer motives from what they know about actors' personalities and goals, past behavior, and the constraints under which they operated. This is exactly how good counterfactuals are constructed.

Historians frequently smuggle counterfactuals into what are alleged to be factual narratives. The English historian E. H. Carr, no friend of counterfactuals, does this in his treatment of the Soviet Union when he insists that Stalin hijacked the Bolshevik Revolution. The implication is that socialism would have developed differently without him. John Lukacs, an even more vitriolic opponent of counterfactuals, does the same in his highly regarded study of the role Churchill played in preventing a British capitulation to Hitler. Lukacs's argument rests on a series of unacknowledged counterfactuals, principally that if Churchill had not become prime minister, the Allies would not have won World War II.

The most plausible counterfactuals rewrite history only minimally. They make small and credible changes in the fabric of history as close as possible in time to the outcome they hope to bring about. A small and credible rewrite of history has the potential over time to bring about a very different world. Consider the survival of the young Elián Gonzalez. In November 1999 Elián fled Cuba with his mother and twelve others in a small boat with a faulty engine; his mother and ten other passengers died in the crossing. Floating in an inner tube, Elián was rescued by two fishermen who handed him over to the US Coast Guard. The subsequent decision by US Attorney General Janet Reno to return Elián to his father in Cuba, rather than allow him to stay with his paternal great uncle in Florida, infuriated many Cuban Americans. Accordingly, many fewer Americans of Cuban descent voted Democratic in the 2000 presidential election. Most Cuban Americans vote Republican, but enough vote Democratic to make a difference. Gore received 25 percent of Florida's Cuban-American votes and John Kerry close to 30 percent in 2004, and Obama won 48 percent in 2008. More Cuban Americans voting for Gore could have made a critical difference in Florida.

If Elián had drowned, Al Gore probably would have won more Cuban-American votes, enough to have carried the state of Florida and become president of the United States. His election would not have forestalled 9/11, but his administration would not have invaded Iraq, a war foisted on the country by the Bush administration for reasons having nothing to do with the terror attacks of 9/11. There was no connection between Al-Qaeda and Saddam Hussein—despite the claims to the contrary by Vice President Cheney—and the Clinton administration had succeeded in largely defanging Saddam through sanctions and no-fly zones. There is good reason to believe that a Gore administration would have continued this policy.

Interconnectedness

Scholars assume, not infrequently, that one aspect of the past can be changed and everything else kept constant. Even plausible rewrites of history can alter the context in a way that renders the consequent moot or undercuts the chain of events leading to it. Richard Nixon lost the 1960 presidential election by the narrowest of margins. Because he was more hawkish than John F. Kennedy, Nixon probably would have ordered an air strike and not a blockade during the Cuban missile crisis. Nor would he have had a secretary of defense like Robert McNamara to make a strong case for restraint. For these same reasons Nixon, in contrast to Kennedy, might have committed US forces to the faltering Bay of Pigs invasion in April 1961. If Castro had been overthrown in 1961, Khrushchev would have had no Communist Cuba to which to send missiles a year later.

Changes we make in the past may require other changes to make them possible and in turn produce changes beyond those we have deliberately introduced. History is like a spring mattress. If one spring is cut or subjected to extra pressure, the others will to varying degrees shift their location and tension. Within reason good counterfactual arguments must specify what else is likely to change as a result of any changes they introduce in the past. In this connection Holger Herwig offers an intriguing counterfactual about World War II: he reasons that Germany could not have won the war even if it had defeated the Soviet Union because Germany, rather than Japan, would then have been the target of the first American atomic weapons. German victory is thus impossible unless some other plausible counterfactual can be devised to derail the Manhattan Project.

Second-Order Counterfactuals

Counterfactuals are complicated by the fact that history's clock does not stop if and when our hypothesized consequent is realized. Subsequent developments can return history to the course, or something close to it, from which the antecedent diverted it. The defeat of the Spanish Armada was a near event; better communication, different decisions by local commanders, or better weather might have allowed the Spanish to land an invasion force in England. If Spain had put an army ashore, it almost certainly would have conquered the country because the English had little organized resistance to offer. Philip II was succeeded by Philip III, a far less capable ruler, who would have had enormous difficulty maintaining an already overextended empire. In relatively short order, England would have thrown off the Spanish yoke.

Attempts to identify and analyze all the counterfactuals arising from the antecedent and consequent would quickly lead to an infinite regress. Researchers must nevertheless try to imagine what events are most likely to unravel the consequent and put history back on the course the counterfactual has moved it away from. The last point entails the recognition that we choose a consequent because of some larger effect it is intended to produce. If developments subsequent to the consequent mitigate its effect, the counterfactual loses its attractiveness. If we could show, for example, that President Al Gore would have invaded Iraq, then the Elián Gonzalez counterfactual is meaningless. No counterfactual argument is complete without some consideration of alternative futures and some assessment of their likelihood and implications for the consequent.

These several rules will not allow us to distinguish empirically valid counterfactuals from those that are not, but they will allow us to weed out poor counterfactuals on the basis of clarity, logic, and substantive completeness. Counterfactuals that survive these tests are more plausible and should appear so to readers.

IMMEDIATE CAUSES OF WAR

The Great War was triggered by twin assassinations at Sarajevo that provided the pretext for Austrian hawks to push for an invasion of Serbia and the grounds for the German kaiser to support them. Austria's ultimatum to Serbia and subsequent declaration of war brought Russia into the war on Serbia's side. Russian military mobilization, for reasons I will explain, triggered a German invasion of Belgium and France. The German invasion of neutral Belgium brought Britain into the war on the side of France. The assassinations were not merely a spark that set dry kindling on fire—the metaphor commonly used by historians to describe this incident and Europe in 1914. They were grave enough incidents in their own right to rupture relations among countries. Austria-Hungary and Germany were the only great powers willing to start a war, and conjuring another scenario in which they might have done so is difficult. This makes these assassinations more tragic because, if Europe had avoided war for only another three years, underlying conditions would have changed in a way to make Austrian, German, and Russian leaders much more risk averse.

Franz Ferdinand Lives

In June 1914 Archduke Franz Ferdinand of Austria-Hungary and his wife, Sophie, made a state visit to Sarajevo to witness Austro-Hungarian army maneuvers at the invitation of General Oskar Potiorek, who also served as governor-general of Bosnia-Herzegovina. The archduke was the nephew and anointed successor (*Thronfolger*) of Franz Josef, emperor of Austria-Hungary. The archduke was also inspector of the army, which was the justification for attending the maneuvers. Sarajevo was the most important city of Bosnia and Herzegovina, which had been unilaterally annexed by Austria in 1908. The annexation provoked a major European crisis and was anathema to Serbia, which had also hoped to incorporate these territories. This move was bold and risky because Serbian resentment was not secret and the Black Hand—an army-sponsored terrorist group—had assassinated King Alexander I of Serbia in 1903.

Reports reached Vienna that Sarajevo was seething with discontent and a dangerous venue for a royal visit. Franz Ferdinand explored the possibility of postponing his trip and seems to have been encouraged by the emperor to do so. The Austrian high command nevertheless decided to proceed with its great maneuvers, and the archduke, given his military responsibility, believed he had no choice but to attend. Duchess Sophie had come to Bosnia with dark misgivings that something dreadful was about to happen to her husband. She was aware that Josip Sunarić, one of the leaders of the Sabor, the Bosnian parliament, had urged General Potiorek to cancel the royal visit because of the local population's hostility to the regime. The evening before the assassination Karl von Rumerskirch, the archduke's chamberlain, pleaded with him to avoid Sarajevo for the same reason. General Potiorek's aide-de-camp, Lieutenant Colonel Eric von Merizzi, interceded and convinced Franz Ferdinand to proceed because cancellation would be a rebuke to his superior, the general. The next morning the archduke and his wife were met at the Sarajevo train station by Potiorek and the lord mayor and ushered into an open touring car to go to a nearby military camp for a quick inspection before going on to city hall. The lead car in the procession was supposed to carry six specially trained security officers but had only three local policemen. On Appel Quay, a long street with houses on one side and an embankment on the other, a young man in a black coat asked a policeman which car carried the archduke and then stepped out into the street to throw a grenade at it. Franz Ferdinand's Czech driver saw something coming his way and accelerated. The bomb fell on the folded roof, rolled off onto the pavement, and exploded under the rear wheel of the next car in the procession. The would-be assassin jumped over the embankment into the river.

Merizzi and a second officer, in the car behind the archduke, were hit by bomb fragments and rushed to a military hospital. Franz Ferdinand dismissed the attack as madness and insisted on proceeding to city hall. Following the ceremony the archduke asked Potiorek if more attacks were likely. Potiorek advised taking a different route and skipping the planned visit to the museum. Other members of the archduke's party urged him to leave Sarajevo immediately, but he insisted on visiting Merizzi in the military hospital and then going on to the museum. The cars drove up Appel Quay, this time at high speed, but the lead car turned into Franz Josef Street by mistake, and the next car, carrying the police guard, followed suit. Franz Ferdinand's driver, in the third car of the procession, was turning to follow when Potiorek ordered the driver to stop, back up, and continue down Appel Quay. Gavrilo Princip, one of the conspirators, was fortuitously positioned at the intersection. He took a revolver out of his coat, and a nearby policeman reached out to grab his hand. An accomplice of Princip struck the policeman, and Princip fired twice at point-blank range into the car in which Franz Ferdinand and Sophie were riding.

Numerous minimal changes in the scenario can readily lead to a different outcome: Princip might have obeyed the order to abort the mission sent to him by the Serbian military conspirators in Belgrade. Austrian authorities in Bosnia might have taken security as seriously as they did the menu and music for the banquets they planned in the archduke's honor. Franz Ferdinand might have canceled his trip in response to multiple warnings and his wife's fears, he might have followed the advice of his advisers and left Sarajevo directly after the ceremony at city hall, or his cavalcade could have adhered to the planned route and raced down Appel Quay past Princip. None of these what-ifs strain our understanding of the world because most royal processions do not stray from their intended routes, and most security details would have rushed the archduke and his wife to safety at the first sign of violence. In this instance, the so-called factual, not the counterfactual, is what strikes us as unrealistic and incredible.

Underlying Causes

Without the assassinations an outbreak of war in the summer of 1914 would have been highly unlikely. Could some other country, or combination of countries, have found another reason to start a war in the months or years ahead? All political parties in Britain were committed to the European status quo, and the Liberal government and Tory opposition were consumed by the Irish problem and the threat of civil war in Ulster. France coveted Alsace-Lorraine but had been on the defensive in Europe since 1871. French politicians and generals perceived their country as increasingly weak compared with Germany. The linchpin of French security was the Franco-Russe alliance, and France supported Russia in 1914 primarily to preserve this alliance. France had also drawn closer to Britain and relied on British military assistance in case of a war with Germany, but the French knew this support would be forthcoming only if they were the victims of a German attack. Italy pursued an aggressive colonial policy that led to war with the Ottoman Empire and also aspired to those parts of Austria-Hungary inhabited by Italian speakers. But before 1914 Italy was constrained by its alliance with Austria and Germany. Italy was also the weakest of the great powers, and there was no public support for war.

In the east the Ottoman Empire was everywhere on the defensive; it was not about to challenge a European power or provide it with a pretext to intervene in support of neighboring Christian peoples in the Balkans. Russia had more or less recovered from its defeat in the Russo-Japanese War of 1904–5 and was intent on expanding its influence in the Balkans. However, Russian leaders did not want war; they mobilized reluctantly in 1914 and hoped, although did not expect, their action would deter Austria from attacking Serbia. Serbia had long-term aspirations to acquire Bosnia-Herzegovina, but Serbia's energies were fully consumed with overcoming the resistance of its newly acquired subjects in Macedonia. In 1910 the German foreign minister Alfred von Kiderlen-Wächter rightly observed, "If we do not conjure up a war into being, certainly no one else will do so."

War was so unlikely in 1914 that we can even speak confidently about preserving the peace in the aftermath of a failed assassination attempt. Suppose that Franz Ferdinand and Sophie had been rushed out of Sarajevo after a bungled assassination attempt, the lead car had not made a wrong turn, Princip was somewhere else in the city, or the policeman's intervention had succeeded. Any of these minimal rewrites of history would have allowed the archduke and archduchess to return home alive from their visit to Sarajevo. Europe was accustomed to failed assassination attempts, and Austria would have found little sympathy in Europe—Germany included—if its leaders had used this attempt as a pretext for war against Serbia. Franz Ferdinand, who was committed to peace with Russia, would almost certainly have opposed such aggression, as would the emperor.

A bungled assassination might have had beneficial consequences. Serbia's diplomatic humiliation in 1909 encouraged the formation of secret societies aimed at undermining Austrian rule in Bosnia-Herzegovina. Colonel Dragutin Dimitrievic, chief of Serbian military intelligence, was code-named Apis as head of the Black Hand, and he was at the center of many of these conspiracies. He supplied arms and other assistance to the archduke's assassins. Serbia's foreign secretary, Nikola Pašić, was hostile to the conspirators but knew of their preparations; he felt constrained to provide only veiled warnings to the Austrian ambassador. Ironically neither Apis nor the other conspirators wanted war with Austria, and Apis did not expect the assassination to provoke one. He hoped to strengthen his hand vis-à-vis civilian authorities and sought to call off the assassination when he became convinced that it would not have this effect. From the perspective of those who mattered in Belgrade, the war was an unintended and undesired consequence of unwanted assassinations. A failed assassination attempt might have allowed the Serbian prime minister and Pašić to rein in Apis, which finally happened in the summer of 1915, when they dismissed him as chief of military intelligence. In December 1916 he was arrested and tried. He was executed the following year.

The principal difference between the Balkan crisis of 1908–9 and the July 1914 crisis was the willingness of Russia to risk war in support of Serbia in 1914. Some historians maintain that Russia was ripe for revolution in 1914 and that World War I postponed the upheaval for three years. If revolution had broken out in the absence of war, Russia might not have been in a position to pursue an aggressive policy in the Balkans. This fate also could have overtaken Austria. Franz Josef died in 1916 and was succeeded by Prince Karl. If Franz Ferdinand had lived, he would have ascended to the throne. Motivated by hatred of Hungarians and the Ausgleich of 1867, which made Hungary an equal partner in the empire, Franz Ferdinand would have sought to reduce Hungary's power. He had considered several strategies toward this end, including a triple rather than dual monarchy to make southern Slavs the third pole in a looser form of federal structure. The documents Franz Ferdinand had prepared for his succession indicate that he probably would have introduced universal suffrage in Hungary at the outset of his reign in the hope of increasing the power of minorities at the expense of the Magyars. This move would have provoked a strong reaction in Budapest, and any further attempts by Franz Ferdinand to undercut the Ausgleich would have raised the prospect of civil war. Even short of armed conflict, the constitutional crisis brought about by any of these measures would have made a war with Serbia a serious and unwanted distraction, not a solution to Austria's domestic problems.

One of the principal causes of war in 1914 was the German military's belief that war was inevitable and had to be fought before 1916 or 1917. Germany faced the prospect of a two-front war: against France in the west and Russia in the east. France and Russia were allies, and both were committed to launching offensives against Germany in any continental war. The German solution to this strategic dilemma was a rapid offensive against France, intended to knock it out of the war before the Russian army could make much headway into Germany in the east. The German general staff reasoned that by 1917 improved Russian mobilization and armaments would compel Germany to give up its long-standing plan of invading France through Belgium at the outset of any European war. Even if the German army defeated the French and advanced on Paris, a Russian army in the east might be closing in on Berlin. One alternative, a direct onslaught on France across the Meuse and

Moselle, had little chance of success because of the terrain and French fortifications. Count Alfred von Schlieffen, chief of the general staff from 1891 to 1906, contemplated such a campaign in 1894 but quickly gave the idea up as unrealistic. Could Germany have conducted an offensive in the east? Russian railway and fortress construction made an Austro-German offensive in Poland difficult but not impossible. However, it could not produce the kind of decisive victory that Helmuth von Moltke sought. If the Germans broached the Narew River line, the Russians could withdraw with relative ease into their vast hinterland. If the Germans followed, they risked the fate of Napoleon in 1812–13.

If German offensives against Russia or France were unrealistic, the most sensible strategy was a defensive posture on both fronts: German generals knew that France and Russia planned to march against Germany at the outbreak of war. If Germany did not invade Belgium, Britain would almost certainly remain neutral. German war games indicated that the French army would fail—as indeed it began to do in 1914—in a series of costly and unsuccessful assaults against the strong German defensive position in Alsace. The war games made it even easier for the Germans to make this expectation self-fulfilling because they generated good information about where to place their forces and what tactics to use to blunt and repel the French offensive.

In the east, the Russian offensive into Prussia was turned back by the meager German forces left in the region. This provides more evidence that a largely defensive strategy was feasible on both the western and eastern fronts. It would also have been politically efficacious. After turning back the French and Russian offensives in our counterfactual world, the Germans could have called for a restoration of peace on the basis of the status quo ante bellum. It seems improbable that the French and Russian governments would have found much support for continuing a war after a series of disheartening defeats, especially if their territories had not been invaded. Nor could these powers have resisted British, and perhaps American, pressures to lay down their arms and accept a reasonable peace. Austria-Hungary would have been preserved, although the Russian empire might have succumbed to revolution. After this defensive German victory, and the presumed collapse of the French and Russian governments that went to war, German military preeminence on the Continent would have been immeasurably strengthened. Berlin would also have gained security from Britain's commitment to keep the peace by preserving the territorial status quo. However, this more sensible approach to German security was anathema to Moltke, who was deeply committed to the offensive on the grounds that it was the only manly strategy.

Moltke constantly tinkered with details of his offensive plan but was unwilling to consider defensive alternatives. Other members of the German general staff doubted the likelihood of victory in 1914, but most clung to the existing Moltke plan because of their collective commitment to the offensive. If war had been avoided in 1914, the contradiction between strategy and reality would have become ever more pronounced. By 1917 Moltke or his successor would have been compelled to abandon plans for war because funds for additional troops were out of the question. As the Germans had not yet developed the concept and technology of the Blitzkrieg, they would have had no viable alternative to the defensive. This is one of the reasons that Moltke and other German generals were so keen for war in 1914.

Military considerations were only one factor in German willingness to risk war in 1914. Moltke and the kaiser also were motivated by their hatred of France and Britain, respectively, and the kaiser was also moved by questions of honor. When Wilhelm pledged German support—undoubtedly the most crucial German decision of the crisis—to Count Alexander Hoyos, Berchtold's friend and Austrian chef de cabinet, at their luncheon meeting on July 5, the kaiser acknowledged Austria's need to preserve its national dignity in the face of an intolerable affront by Serbia. Serbian officials were indeed responsible for the assassination plot, although they had acted behind the back of their government. More than two weeks later, Wilhelm was still furious at Serbia, writing in the margin of a cable, "Serbia is nothing but a band of robbers that must be seized for its crimes! I will meddle in nothing of which the Emperor [Franz Josef] is alone competent to judge!" The next day the kaiser penned another revealing observation: "In *vital* questions and those of honor, one does not consult with others." On July 6 in Kiel, the kaiser made an interesting confession to his friend, Krupp von Bohlen und Halbach. Wilhelm told the steel magnate, "This time I shall not cave in"—and repeated himself three times. Perhaps Sarajevo had also become a matter of personal honor for Wilhelm, eager to convince himself and others that he was a man of courage. Moltke did not have the power or influence to bring about war on his own or even with the support of German chancellor Theobald von Bethmann Hollweg. The kaiser's position was critical, and it seems unlikely, given his caution in previous crises, that he would have assumed the risk involved in unreservedly backing Austria if not for the assassinations that made honor foremost in his mind. He framed his role in the crisis as serving as a second to Franz-Josef in his forthcoming duel with Serbia.

To this point I have asked whether a European war could have been delayed, or perhaps altogether avoided, in the absence of the twin assassinations at Sarajevo. Could it have come *sooner?* I am inclined to discount this prospect. Austria considered and rejected going to war with Serbia in December 1912, April–May 1913, and October 1913. Between 1905 and 1914 the kaiser and his chancellors spurned Moltke's repeated pleas to exploit great power crises as pretexts for war. Austrian and German swords remained sheathed because political leaders in Vienna and Berlin saw war as politically and militarily risky and did not feel threatened enough to assume these risks.

SARAJEVO REVISITED

In contrast to the historians who see the Sarajevo assassinations as a mere pretext, the historian Joachim Remak insists that "Sarajevo was more than an excuse for war, it was one of its major causes." Many reasons can be adduced in support. Arguably the most important was the assassination itself and the political challenge to Austria-Hungary that it constituted. In June 1914 the Austrian prime minister Berchtold, with Emperor Franz Josef's support, began a diplomatic offensive to bolster the empire's position in the Balkans and frustrate Triple Entente efforts to build a new Balkan League. No one was talking about war. The assassination transformed the situation. Chief of staff Conrad von Hötzendorf pushed for war, and other officials in the Austrian foreign office and military argued that failure to respond forcibly would undermine, if not destroy, the empire's standing as a great power and embolden its domestic and foreign enemies. For Franz Josef, Sarajevo also had a personal dimension: he was outraged by the assassination of a member of the royal family and accepted the need to make war to preserve the honor of the empire. He was by no means confident of the outcome and told Conrad, "If we must go under, we better go under decently." Kaiser Wilhelm also grieved the loss of Franz Ferdinand, whom he considered a friend and had spent time with only two weeks before.

Wilhelm wanted Austria to move against Serbia to show that actions against legitimate rulers would not be tolerated.

Sarajevo shifted the balance of power in Vienna. Franz Ferdinand's views on defense matters were almost as important as those of the emperor. The archduke's influence derived from his official status as successor to the throne (*Thronfolger*), from his interest in and knowledge of military affairs, and from the extensive network of contacts he had cultivated throughout the armed forces. His decidedly peaceful orientation evolved during the Balkan wars. The Thronfolger was intent on extending Austrian influence in the Balkans but not at the risk of war with Russia. He warned, "A war between Austria and Russia would end either with the overthrow of the Romanovs or with the overthrow of the Habsburgs—or perhaps the overthrow of both." He cherished the idea of monarchical solidarity in the form of some revival of the Holy Alliance and had continually sought to cultivate good relations with Nicholas II. On a more practical level Franz Ferdinand took Russian military capability more seriously than either the Austrian war minister or chief of staff and was convinced that war against Serbia would draw in Russia. The archduke did not believe that the Austro-Hungarian army was ready for war, and he worried that Italy would defect from the Triple Alliance and Germany would find some reason to stand aloof. More fundamentally Franz Ferdinand opposed war because it would make it impossible for him to impose fundamental changes on the structure of the empire once he took the throne.

Consider the following counterfactual: If the governor-general of Bosnia-Herzegovina, Oskar Potiorek, had been killed at Sarajevo instead of Franz Ferdinand, Vienna would have responded differently. Like Conrad, Potiorek was keen for war, and his death would have removed another supporter of military action from the scene. More important, Franz Ferdinand would have remained influential in shaping Austria's foreign policy. His opposition to war, together with that of Hungarian prime minister István Tisza, the senior voice against war in June and early July 1914, would have carried considerable weight because the two men were otherwise at odds. Tisza was the great defender of Hungary, and Franz Ferdinand made no secret of his dislike of Tisza and of Hungarians more generally. With Franz Ferdinand and Tisza urging moderation, Berchtold, a weak personality, also would have pursued a cautious line, and Franz Josef, cross-pressured in 1914, might well have sided with them instead of with Conrad. Hoyos would not have undertaken a mission to seek German support for war against Serbia; Berlin would have been consulted with a diplomatic end in mind. The channel for communication with Germany would not have been the hawks in the Austrian foreign office but Franz Ferdinand. He had close personal relations with Kaiser Wilhelm and had been used in the past to sound out Berlin's intentions in the Balkans. Merely changing the victims of the terrorist attack in Sarajevo might have been enough to alter in a fundamental way Austria-Hungary's response.

Sarajevo provided a necessary incentive and opportunity for Germany. Moltke had pushed for war almost from the moment he became chief of staff because he was committed to attacking France and thought a successful war would promote traditional values of honor and service within Germany. He wanted to go to war while Germany still had a chance of victory in a conflict that he knew would bring Russia in on France's side. Although the German general staff had low regard for the military prowess of their Austrian ally, they were horrified at the prospect of an Austrian decline because it would leave Russia free to concentrate all its forces against Germany in East Prussia. In Berlin the assassination was perceived as threatening Austria's standing as a great power because it might expose Austria's lack of will to act like one. This additional consideration, when weighed along with the general concern for the deteriorating military balance, made Chancellor Bethmann Hollweg more receptive to Moltke's pleas for action.

Bethmann Hollweg was more prescient than most of his contemporaries in recognizing that, as he put it, a European war was likely to topple more thrones than it would prop up. He accordingly deemed the backing of the Social Democrats, the largest and best-organized working-class organization in Europe, the sine qua non for military action. Without confidence in the support of the Social Democrats, the chancellor would not have taken his "leap into the dark." Moltke knew this and in February 1913 had discouraged Conrad from attacking Serbia on the grounds that the German people would not support a war that Austria had provoked against a seemingly conciliatory adversary. Sarajevo was a provocation tailor made for Bethmann Hollweg. The assassinations aroused considerable sympathy for Austria throughout Europe, not least among the German working class. Although the politically sophisticated widely regarded the Austrian ultimatum as heavy handed, ordinary Germans perceived their country as a bystander in a Balkan conflict and then the innocent target of Russian aggression. Chancellor Bethmann Hollweg played to these sentiments and benefited greatly from the fear and dislike of Russia among Social Democrats, who regarded the czarist regime as barbaric because of its treatment of labor, dissident intellectuals, and its religious and ethnic minorities. The result was the Burgfrieden, or domestic peace, of August 4 in which the Social Democrats voted with near unanimity for funding for the war.

Sarajevo created the psychological environment necessary for Kaiser Wilhelm and the chancellor to overcome their inhibitions about war. The German admiral Alfred von Tirpitz observed, "When the Emperor did not consider the peace to be threatened he liked to give full play to his reminiscences of famous ancestors, [but] in moments which he realized to be critical he proceeded with extraordinary caution." To his contemporaries the chancellor came across as a fatalist, a man who had a deep revulsion for war but felt powerless to oppose the prevalent view that it was necessary. Kaiser and chancellor were caught on the horns of a dilemma: Germany would benefit from a diplomatic triumph that would break up the Franco-Russe alliance, but this could be achieved—if it could be achieved at all—only by risking war. Neither man was willing to accept responsibility for starting a European war. Until July 1914 they procrastinated, a hallmark of defensive avoidance. By deferring a decision that was too difficult for them to make, kaiser and chancellor preserved their psychological equilibrium. The July crises offered them a way out of their dilemma.

When Hoyos met Wilhelm and Bethmann Hollweg on July 5 in Potsdam, he asked only for their support *if* Russia threatened to intervene in support of Serbia. Kaiser and chancellor expected Russia to back down as it had in the Bosnian crisis of 1909, and this was also the expectation of their ambassador in St. Petersburg. They doubted France would come to Russia's assistance, that Britain would intervene if France did, or that British intervention would matter militarily. German support for Austria precipitated its ultimatum and declaration of war against Serbia, Russia's subsequent mobilization against Austria, German ultimatums to Russia and France, and German mobilization, which were the equivalent of war. When kaiser and chancellor confronted Russian mobilization or, more accurately, premature and exaggerated reports of Russian mobilization that flooded the channels of German military intelligence, they convinced themselves that they were only reacting to Russian initiatives and that St. Petersburg, not they, bore responsibility for the war they were about to unleash.

To recapitulate: the Sarajevo assassinations changed the political and psychological environment in Vienna and Berlin in six important ways, all of which may have been necessary for the decisions that led to war. The assassinations:

- Constituted a political challenge to which Austrian leaders believed they had to respond forcefully; anything less would encourage further challenges by domestic and foreign enemies.
- Shocked and offended Franz Josef and Kaiser Wilhelm and made both emperors more receptive to calls for decisive measures to preserve Austria's honor and its standing as a great power.
- Changed the policymaking context in Vienna by removing the principal spokesman for peace.
- May have been the catalyst for Chancellor Bethmann Hollweg's new willingness to risk war.
- Made it possible for Bethmann Hollweg to win the support of the Socialists, without which he would not have risked war.
- Created a psychological environment in which Wilhelm and Bethmann Hollweg could proceed toward war in incremental steps, convincing themselves at the outset that their actions were unlikely to provoke a European war and, at the end of the crisis, that others were responsible for war.

A striking feature of the July crisis was the tremendous psychological difficulty German leaders had in making a decision for war. Given their unwillingness to accept responsibility for starting a great power war, it is difficult to imagine how kaiser and chancellor could have authorized mobilization if they had been compelled to recognize their responsibility for war from the outset. If the archduke had not been assassinated, giving Austrian hawks a desired pretext for war, Germany might have reached the fateful year of 1917 still at peace with its neighbors. Its leaders might have found that their fears of a window of vulnerability were greatly exaggerated, and that their adversaries were constrained from attacking Germany for many of the same reasons that had prevented Germany from seizing an opportunity for war in the decade before 1914.

3

The Best Plausible World

TO BRING ABOUT OUR BETTER COUNTERFACTUAL WORLD, Europe would have had to avoid war in 1914 as well as in the decade that followed. This would have required the leaders of Austria, Germany, and Russia to become more risk averse. Beyond preventing war in 1914, I argue that no additional counterfactuals are necessary to bring this change about. If a Continental war could have been avoided for only three years more, leaders of all three empires would have become increasingly risk averse in response to the changing circumstances at home and abroad. The importance of other underlying causes of war would have diminished in the longer term, possibly paving the way for a more peaceful, productive, culturally vibrant Europe.

PREVENTING CONFLUENCE

Willingness to take risks in 1914 was the product of three sets of causes. First and foremost was Germany's security dilemma, caused by the prospect of a two-front war: against France in the west and Russia in the east. The general staff worried that every year their forces were becoming less able to defeat their adversaries sequentially. Meanwhile a series of developments in the Balkans threatened the external security and internal stability of Austria-Hungary. These developments encouraged influential political and military leaders to consider war with Serbia as a way to counter these threats. The third set of factors was centered in St. Petersburg and was a confluence of external setbacks (defeat in the Russo-Japanese War of 1904–5, humiliation in the Bosnian annexation crisis of 1909) and internal weaknesses (the revolution of 1905, growing alienation of the middle classes, rise of a powerful revolutionary movement). These concerns combined to make Russian leaders fearful of the costs, at home and abroad, of another foreign policy defeat.

The German predicament was very much the product of Moltke's war plan. It called for Germany to invade and defeat France before Russian forces could penetrate too deeply into eastern Prussia. This was always a high-risk plan, all the more so after Russia, thanks to French loans, began to build more railways to mobilize the army more quickly. By 1914 Moltke and the general staff were worried that ongoing Russian rearmament and railway construction would allow Russian forces to penetrate deep into Prussia while the German army was engaged in France. Moltke wanted war now rather than later and consistently exaggerated his confidence in his war plan in conversations with the kaiser, chancellor, and foreign minister. Their erroneous belief that victory required an early war significantly shaped their response to Austria's request for support in July 1914.

France gave financial support to Russia in the hope of restraining Germany. French leaders reasoned that Berlin's fear of the consequences of a two-front war would make the Germans more cautious. Instead, the French loans to the Russians helped to provoke the German invasion they were intended to forestall. Something similar happened with Russia in 1914. Its leaders authorized mobilization in the hope of restraining Germany and Austria, not to provide a casus belli.

Austrian leaders worried about a Balkan League that would constitute an external threat and fan nationalist and separatist sentiment within their empire. Conrad and Berchtold wanted to exploit the assassination of Franz Ferdinand as a pretext for attacking Serbia, in large part to show Serbia who was boss. Franz Josef was persuaded to go along on the grounds that attacking was necessary to uphold Austria's honor and that Berlin was now willing to offer support.

The Russians knew nothing about these developments and behaved in ways that exacerbated Austro-German insecurities. Wilhelm, Bethmann Hollweg, and Foreign Secretary Gottlieb von Jagow deluded themselves into thinking that they might repeat the success of 1909—when the German threat of mobilization forced Russia to back down in the Bosnian annexation crisis—and compel Russia to remain on the sidelines of an Austro-Serb war. But the humiliation of 1909 had prompted a Russian commitment to not back down again, as the Russians feared any further sign of weakness would encourage domestic and foreign adversaries to doubt Russian resolve and invite further challenges. The commitment to this policy was strengthened by a cabinet reshuffle in 1914. These several gestalt shifts entirely changed the nature and outcome of great power interactions.

One of the most remarkable features of 1914 was the coincidental timing of the German and Austrian security problems and the intensification of their respective fears. Although Russia was a common threat, each ally's security problems had largely independent causes, and they became acute at the same time for no particular reason. Germany's security dilemma was the result of its geographic position, previous policies that had encouraged its two most powerful neighbors to ally against it, and above all its commitment to an offensive military strategy. Russia's improved military and mobilization capability, the developments that so threatened Germany in 1914, were the result of Russian industrialization and access to French capital markets. German willingness to risk war was also the result of the perceived decline of Austria-Hungary, Germany's principal military ally. German political and military authorities worried that failure to support Austria in 1914—indeed to encourage it to take dramatic action—would only accelerate its decline and leave Germany at the mercy of Russia and France.

Austria-Hungary's insecurity was the result of its relative decline as a great power. In 1815, following the defeat of Napoleon, Austria-Hungary was at the peak of its power. In 1848 it was wracked by revolution, in 1859 it lost a war to the Piedmont and France, and in 1866 it was defeated by Prussia and excluded from any further influence in Germany. Austria-Hungary was widely regarded as militarily weak and internally divided. The precipitous decline of the Ottoman Empire paradoxically intensified Austrian insecurity. Ottoman weakness encouraged the Italians' occupation of Tripoli in September 1911. The ensuing war between the Ottomans and Italy provided the opportunity for Serbia, Bulgaria, and Greece to take up arms, and to almost everyone's surprise, their ragtag armies all but expelled the Ottomans from Europe. Serbia doubled its population and territory, and, backed by Russia, it sought to revive the Balkan League and transform it into an anti-Austrian alliance. The emergence of an adversary on their southern flank and Serbia's perceived ability to stimulate nationalism among southern Slavic peoples in the Austro-Hungarian Empire made Austria's leaders insecure.

Russia's problem was similar. It had suffered defeat at the hands of Japan in 1904–5, underwent a nearly successful revolution in its aftermath, and suffered another humiliation in the Bosnian annexation crisis of 1909. This crisis arose from Austria-Hungary's unilateral incorporation of Bosnia and Herzegovina, and German support for Austria compelled a much weaker Russia to give up its opposition without receiving any kind of quid pro quo. Such foreign setbacks weakened the Russian regime at home and made its leaders feel acutely threatened.

German leaders did not feel so threatened in the decade leading up to 1914; German chancellors rejected military demands for war in 1905 and 1912 and supported diplomatic resolution of the 1912 and 1913 crises that threatened war between Austria and Serbia, and Austria and Montenegro, respectively. If the Italians had not occupied Tripoli, or if the Balkan events that Austria-Hungary found so threatening had happened a few years earlier, the German kaiser and chancellor probably would not have encouraged Austria to attack Serbia. Nor would the Germans have felt so threatened if these events had occurred a few years later. Timing was everything in 1914, and for this reason alone, World War I was highly contingent.

Each development that threatened Germany, Austria, and Russia was contingent. These developments were the result of human decisions—in general avoidable ones—that had the unintended consequence of dividing Europe into two armed and hostile camps. If Otto von Bismarck had been able to persuade Kaiser Wilhelm I not to annex Alsace-Lorraine, the Germans might have avoided enduring French hostility. If Bismarck's successors had managed relations with Russia more successfully, its leaders would not have had a strong incentive to ally with France. If Moltke and the German general staff had been prepared to adopt a defensive strategy, the fear of strategic disadvantage would have disappeared because Germany would no longer have a single war plan that involved invading France. Alternatively the Anglo-French understanding (the Entente Cordiale), which brought Britain into the war on France's side, could easily have been prevented by a kaiser who kept his mouth shut on several key occasions and never sanctioned the unnecessary expense of a counterproductive naval buildup. The latter led to a naval race with Britain and convinced its leaders and public opinion of Germany's aggressive intentions.

Austro-Serb relations were severely aggravated by Austria-Hungary's annexation of Bosnia and Herzegovina in 1908. Austria-Hungary's chief of staff, Conrad von Hötzendorf, had been pushing for annexation for some time and convinced Alois Lexa von Aehrenthal, who became foreign minister in 1906, to take this step as part of a new, assertive policy in the Balkans. Aehrenthal's poorly conceived initiative provoked a crisis by humiliating Russia and deeply embittering the Serbs. The annexation crisis destroyed a decade of Austro-Russian cooperation and put the two eastern empires on a collision course. Had Vienna had a more cautious and far-sighted foreign minister, it would have avoided this clash and managed the Austro-Russian rivalry as effectively as it had been in the past. If so, Russia would have been more restrained and probably would not have violated the tacit agreement between the two empires not to support dissident groups within each other's territory or sphere of influence. St. Petersburg intensified this tension by stoking Romanian nationalism in Transylvania with the goal of detaching the country from its not so secret alliance with Austria. In the long run Slavic nationalism would have asserted itself, encouraging the Slovene, Croat, and Serb populations along the southern flank of Austria-Hungary to demand greater autonomy, if not independence. In the north Czechs were already involved in a culture war with the

German population to gain equal status for their language. National struggle of this kind, although threatening to the long-term survival of the Austro-Hungarian Empire, could have been managed for some time. As late as 1914, relatively few voices were calling for independence. The division of Europe into two militarily powerful but insecure alliance systems was neither inevitable nor made war unavoidable.

IT SEEMED THE PEACE WOULD GO ON AND ON

The ninety-nine years from the end of the Napoleonic Wars in 1815 to the outbreak of Continental war in 1914 was the most peaceful in Europe's history, marked by economic development and sustained optimism about progress. Famines disappeared in western Europe, as did pandemics. The benefits of industrialism had finally begun to outweigh its initial heavy costs in workers' lives and well-being. Living standards were rising, by an average of 1 percent a year between 1870 and 1900 in Britain. Education was becoming more widespread, death rates for children were dropping, and adult workers were living longer. In Germany and Britain, Tory politicians like Bismarck and Benjamin Disraeli had gained political popularity from reaching out to the working class through social legislation. The rise of trade unions and Socialist parties on the Continent and in Britain brought more benefits to the working class. Death from infection was also declining as a result of more effective public health measures.

The period from 1815 to 1914 marked the first time Europe had seen more years of peace than war. The several great power wars—German unification (1864, 1866, 1870–71) and Italian unification (1848, 1859)—were fought for limited objectives and were of limited duration. The exception was the three-year Crimean War (1853–56).

It nevertheless consisted of a series of short, if acute, engagements on land and sea and the yearlong siege of Sevastopol.

Significant progress had also been made internationally. Common action by the great powers had suppressed slavery. Legal restrictions were lifted against Catholics, dissenters, and Jews in Britain, and religious and ethnic minorities in western Europe generally improved their positions. International law had all but eliminated piracy. British and German business, shipping, and banking elites established a dense web of professional and personal relationships, strengthened by intermarriage. War among the industrial powers was increasingly regarded as irrational, if not economically suicidal, although all continued to spend large sums on their armed forces. Britain and Germany were engaged in a costly naval race to produce expensive, armor-plated battleships of the *Dreadnought* class.

Despite the Anglo-German arms race, the public and leaders alike considered war less likely than in the past. European public opinion was increasingly antiwar, and this included colonial violence. The Napoleonic and American civil wars had spawned numerous peace societies on both sides of the Atlantic. Liberals everywhere came to regard peace as the handmaiden to wealth because it provided a more predictable and less disruptive environment that encouraged investment and trade. The two Hague conferences, of 1899 and 1907, took significant steps to limit the destructiveness of warfare. A third, planned for 1915 and derailed by World War I, was to have addressed the possibility of substituting arbitration for war. The Hague conferences, the Olympic Games, the first renewal of which was held in 1896, enthusiasm for Volapük and Esperanto as international languages of peace, the growth of cross-border travel, and the understanding it seemed to bring in its wake fanned the hopes of progressives that international relations might become increasingly governed by law. In 1849 the American poet Ralph Waldo Emerson felt confident enough to proclaim, "War is on its last legs and a universal peace is as sure as is the prevalence of civilization over barbarism." In 1899 the Austrian baroness Bertha von Sutter published an antiwar novel, *Die Waffen Nieder!* (Down with Arms), that quickly became an international best seller and won her the Nobel Peace Prize in 1905. In 1910 Norman Angel, another best-selling author who would win a Nobel Prize, made a compelling case that territorial conquest could no longer augment national wealth.

In Germany public opinion was also antiwar, although nationalist sentiment was high in the aftermath of the 1911 Agadir crisis, in which Germany unsuccessfully challenged France's supremacy in Morocco. In the second decade of the twentieth century, war was far from inevitable. Europe could just have readily continued its peaceful course, and the longer peace lasted, the more enduring it was likely to become. How different would Europe and the world have become in this peaceful alternative world? In my optimistic scenario, Europe enjoys decades of sustained economic development. Eastern Europe, not held back by two world wars and Communism, begins to pull abreast of the West sooner rather than later. Russia undergoes a revolution, loses most of its empire, and is governed by a quasi-authoritarian but capitalist regime. Like the countries of the Pacific rim in the late twentieth century, Russia and most of its successor states gradually evolve into more stable regimes as the result of economic prosperity and the emergence of a large, educated middle class and export-oriented business elite. Austria-Hungary survives but, under pressure from dissident nationalities and a democratic Germany, adopts a federal structure in the face of Magyar opposition.

More serious threats to the peace could have arisen in central, eastern, and southern Europe. The Austro-Hungarian, Russian, and Ottoman Empires faced serious nationality problems. In the late eighteenth century Poland had been divided and absorbed into Prussia, Austria, and Russia, and Poles had periodically risen up against their overlords. Austria-Hungary was a polyglot state in which Germans and Hungarians ruled over increasingly resentful Czechs, Slovaks, Italians, Slovenes, Croats, Serbs, and Bosnians. Finns, Estonians, Lithuanians, Latvians, and Ukrainians were among those who dreamed about the dissolution of the Russian Empire. The Ottomans were in decline but retained a toehold in Europe. All four empires would disappear by 1918, giving rise to a score of newly independent states. Some of these states would clash over disputed territory. The ethnic cleansing and wars that followed the breakup of Yugoslavia, one of these successor states, is but the latest iteration of this violence.

With no World War I, the three eastern empires survive. Their evolution is unpredictable. In the most benign scenario Austria-Hungary becomes a federal state in which the southern Slavs become more equal partners with the Germans and Hungarians. Czechs, Slovaks, Poles, and Italians gain considerable autonomy. Franz Ferdinand envisaged a solution along these lines and, as a first step toward this goal, intended to extend the franchise when he assumed office. Electoral reform would have put him on a collision course with the Hungarians, whose aristocracy dominated Slavic and Romanian hinterlands, but the Hungarians would have lost their control in any fair election. Had Austria-Hungary weathered this constitutional crisis, it might have moved further in the direction of a constitutional monarchy. A civil war, pitting Hungarians against Germans and Slavs, would have fractured the empire.

Austria's fate rested partly in German hands even though relations between the two countries had never been easy or close. Bismarck made war against Austria in 1866 as a necessary step toward unification of Germany under Prussian auspices. In the aftermath he did his best to patch up relations. Bismarck's successors alienated Russia, which allied with France, compelling the Germans to ally with Austria. The Germans treated Vienna as the junior partner in this alliance but had strong incentives to forestall Austria's decline. Berlin's only other ally, Italy, was rightly regarded as unreliable and made German leaders even more paranoid about encirclement by France and Russia, and perhaps Britain.

Kaiser Wilhelm and Chancellor Bethmann Hollweg would have used all of Germany's political and economic clout to forestall fragmentation of Austria-Hungary. This might have involved pressure on the new emperor to back away from his reforms. Alternatively the Germans might have provided support for a more federal system that recognized the cultural and political rights of other nationalities. The latter option is less likely, as kaiser and chancellor alike had fundamentally conservative instincts. They also would have worried about the consequences for Germany, which had restive Polish, French, and Danish minorities. The Germans might nevertheless have swallowed hard and supported some kind of federal solution if it appeared to be the only way to save their ally.

Germany faced its own constitutional crisis because of military interference in civilian affairs and other undemocratic aspects of its political system. The outcome of this struggle would determine whether Germany would evolve into a full-fledged constitutional democracy or become even more authoritarian, with the reins of power firmly in military and aristocratic hands.

The Zabern affair of 1913 revealed the extent of German unrest. Two battalions of Prussian infantry were garrisoned in the town of Zabern, and a pathologically aggressive second lieutenant provoked widespread protests by insulting the largely French Alsatian population. Military authorities overreacted and resorted to extralegal repressive measures. They arrested and held overnight people who happened to be in the vicinity, including a local judge. Higher military authorities defended the behavior of their underlings and insisted on their right to supersede civilian authorities and impose military law when they thought it necessary. The resulting upheaval provoked a heated debate in the Reichstag about the power of the military and censure of the government. Only the year before, the Social Democratic Party (SPD) had won 34.8 percent of the vote, becoming the largest party in the Reichstag with 27.7 percent of its seats. Between 1907 and 1911 a Center-Left alliance of the SPD, Center (Zentrum) Party, and other progressives had emerged. SPD and Zentrum had both opposed and accommodated the political system Bismarck brought into being. After the 1912 election the SPD was buoyed by the electorate's dissatisfaction with the status quo. In January 1913 it rejected the government's policy of expropriating Polish land to resettle German peasants and increase the German percentage of the population. In December, following the events in Zabern, the Reichstag, in a rare show of solidarity, voted overwhelmingly to censure the government. If peace had endured, and the army and government had continued to behave as provocatively and unwisely—which we can be sure they would have—the SPD and Zentrum might have been able to muster majorities for significant democratic reforms.

Given another decade or two of peace, Germany could have evolved into a constitutional democracy. The principal mechanism for this transformation would have been the refusal of the Reichstag to authorize the military budget. The National Liberals had provoked a constitutional crisis in 1862 by withholding budgetary approval, but Bismarck outmaneuvered and divided them by provoking a war with Denmark as a first step toward national unification. This time reformers were in a much stronger position, but national unification still had many backers. Most National Liberals opted for unification over democracy in 1864, and the Social Democrats bowed to nationalism in 1914. Only four members of the Reichstag voted against the Burgfrieden, which established a party truce and credits for the war. Affiliated trade unions agreed not to strike. The trade union movement was nevertheless strong, and the Social Democrats were not the only political party interested in democratic reforms. Heavy-handed repression by the government in peacetime would only have increased their commitment.

Let us return to our counterfactual world. If Austria-Hungary's resolution of its nationality crisis depended in part on Germany's response, Germany's transition to democracy depended on external assistance from Britain and France. The Reichstag's refusal to appropriate funds for the army in 1920 would have provoked the immediate countercharge from the kaiser and general staff that irresponsible Socialists and their parliamentary allies were putting the nation's security at risk. The prospect of arms control would have undercut the propaganda war against the Socialists. In this scenario Britain then offers another round of negotiations to end the naval arms race and expresses willingness to consider a mutual downsizing of the British and German battle fleets. Admiral Tirpitz and the German Navy League are vehemently opposed, but London undercuts their appeals to the public by announcing a unilateral cut in the military ship-building budget. This decision is relatively risk free because Britain has a much larger fleet and plenty of time to resume its building program if Berlin fails to follow suit. The Reichstag responds positively, as it has every incentive to do in a constitutional crisis. The kaiser and navy have to settle for a reduced fleet or no funding.

London encourages Paris to follow its example, and the French Left is delighted by the prospect of deep cuts in military spending. Almost everyone in France considers Alsace-Lorraine part of the national patrimony and resents its loss to Germany in the aftermath of the 1870–71 Franco-Prussian War. In the fifty years since, the French people have become accustomed to the new status quo, and while France still has a romantic yearning for reunification, no one supports risking, let alone fighting, a revanchist war. The French army is nevertheless committed to launching an offensive to regain Alsace-Lorraine at the outset of any war. This strategy is utterly unrealistic, as the terrain is hilly and easily defended and would reduce the size of French defenses in the north, where the Germans are expected to launch an invasion, perhaps through Belgium.

The German military is much more concerned about the French and Russian armies than about the British fleet. For no reason German military and political leaders have convinced themselves that Britain will remain neutral in any Continental war, and they dismiss the small British army as, in any case, irrelevant to the outcome. Although the German general staff considers the possibility of a long war, and Moltke more or less expects one, they fail to analyze the critical role British ground and naval forces will play in any extended conflict. The Schlieffen Plan calls for an invasion of France and the encirclement of Paris before advancing Russian armies penetrate too deeply into German territory in the east. Berlin would find most welcome a significant reduction of either opposing army.

A French army downsizing can take place only as part of a negotiated package, although the Center-Left French government, urged on by Britain, initiates a small reduction of its forces by calling up fewer young men for the next year. It challenges Germany to reciprocate. Once again the possibility of transnational parliamentary cooperation arises in the form of negotiated French-German reductions in military expenditures forced, if necessary, on an otherwise unyielding kaiser and general staff. Parliamentarians on both sides know that any kind of mutual reduction of forces—and especially one in which Russia participates—will significantly reduce Continental tensions. It will also strengthen prodemocracy forces in Germany. German and French Socialists, and all British political parties, are peacefully inclined, as are many of their colleagues in Austria-Hungary and Italy. They recognize that the longer peace prevails, the stronger pro-peace forces will become, making it increasingly difficult to sustain the level of pre-1914 great power military spending. The United States spends even less on its armed forces and calls a conference on arms reductions. Socialists in all the major European countries respond enthusiastically, as they all seek to shift spending on the military to social and other needs. A virtuous cycle of peace and arms control is gradually made self-fulfilling, based on the widespread expectations of peace that historically prevailed until August 1914.

Russia remains the most problematic of the great European powers. In 1914 it was the largest but least developed of the powers. It had the smallest middle and working classes and the most authoritarian government. Supposing that Russia would have evolved peacefully into a democracy supportive of the status quo is not reasonable. This did not happen in the far more developed Russia in the decades following the collapse of Communism and the Soviet Union. The most optimistic scenario we can reasonably expect is a somewhat less authoritarian regime in which the Duma gradually increases its powers. Western investment and perhaps aid tied to democratization hasten the growth of parliamentary power. A more recalcitrant tsarist regime resists all reform, and revolution breaks out again, as it did in 1905 after Russia's defeat by Japan. Russia is weakened by civil disorder, raising the prospect of the empire's dissolution. This happened in 1918 and again in 1991 after Boris Yeltsin proclaimed the independence of Russia from the Soviet Union. Most nationalities along the empire's peripheries quickly proclaim their independence.

In 1914, as in 1991, dissident nationalities constituted an almost unbroken chain, from the Finns and Baltic peoples in the north to the Poles, White Russians, and Ukrainians in the west and south to diverse ethnic groups in the Caucasus and Central Asia. In 1918 the German military junta, hoping to make major territorial and economic gains and become stronger in relation to its Western enemies, encouraged the breakup of the Russian Empire. The 1917 Russian Revolution and the Bolshevik coup that followed led to a costly civil war, in which the western Allies and Japan supported the ultimately unsuccessful anti-Bolshevik forces and rebellious nationalities. In our better world a Kerensky-style coalition regime receives immediate European support, reducing the chances of a successful Bolshevik coup. More important, Russia is not at war for three years. The Bolsheviks would not have had the opportunity to build large-scale support by characterizing themselves as the party of bread and peace—in contrast to the Kerensky government's commitment to continue fighting on the side of the Allies. With the Bolsheviks marginalized, the Mensheviks and Social Revolutionaries are the dominant Socialist parties, making possible parliamentary coalitions and democratic government.

The timing of the Russian Empire's breakup is important in avoiding war. If Russia is thrown into turmoil by revolution and civil war before any significant movement toward accommodation and arms control by the other great powers, it could threaten the European peace. In the better world Russia's turmoil is delayed, but the revolution and the possibility of Polish independence arouse sympathy and trigger similar desires for independence in Polish citizens of Prussia and Austria-Hungary. The two empires respond by creating a rump Polish state that includes the Polish populated lands of the former Russian Empire, with Warsaw as its capital. Vienna and Berlin attempt to satisfy their Polish minorities with concessions of greater cultural autonomy. Ukrainian independence from Russia arouses nationalism among Ukrainians in Austria-Hungary. It provokes a conflict with Poland, as the two nationalities are partly intermingled, and Polish nationalists had far-reaching and entirely unrealistic territorial goals. Ukrainian nationalists begin ethnic cleansing of Poles from territory they claim.

Even in the most optimistic scenario, some eastern European nationalities remain bitter antagonists, and the breakup of the Russian Empire is accompanied by escalating violence. As with the breakup of Yugoslavia in the historical world, the Western powers are primarily concerned with avoiding a wave of refugees seeking entry into their countries and do what they can, short of direct military involvement, to bring about a political solution. In the Yugoslav case, televised and well-reported atrocities forced the hand of Western governments; the North American Treaty Organization (NATO) conducted airstrikes that halted Serbian armor and were the catalyst for the Dayton peace talks. In the better world there is no direct intervention but considerable diplomatic pressure, which has less immediate effect. Only after lengthy fighting and a stalemate are the great powers able to arrange a cease-fire and provisional borders. Tensions remain high in the east, and the negotiated political solution is inherently unstable.

Italy is the other great European power, a status conceded to it by the great powers as a matter of courtesy. Italy had a sizable population—about 35 million on the eve of the First World War—but its literacy rate was low, and malaria and pellagra were endemic to its countryside. The Italian peninsula was almost entirely lacking in coal, compelling the importation of fuel from Britain. Steel output was a mere fraction of that of Britain or Germany, and the rail network was far less dense. Italy was plagued by deep divisions between north and south, the continuing prominence of dialects, and a political system that led to frequent changes in government and parliamentary gridlock. Italy was allied with Austria-Hungary and Germany but claimed territory that was part of Austria. This comprises what would become, after 1918, the Veneto, Venezia-Fruili-Guilia, and Trentino-Alto Adige, that is, much of northern Italy. After being promised these lands as the fruits of victory, Rome allied with the Entente Cordiale in World War I.

World War I strengthened right-wing nationalist forces in Italy. The country entered the conflict in May 1915 and paid an enormous human price for the territories it received at the Versailles peace settlement. The Italian middle class was nearly ruined by the postwar inflation, dramatic increases in the price of coal, high unemployment, and a growing trade imbalance. The peasant struggle for land became increasingly desperate, and industrial unrest became more acute and violent. Giuseppe Mazzini's vision of a modernizing Left-oriented republic lost ground to a cruder form of nationalism, personified by poet, journalist, soldier Gabriele D'Annunzio and Benito Mussolini. In making his own bid for power, Mussolini, a Socialist turned nationalist, distanced himself from D'Annunzio. Mussolini appealed to Italian anger at the so-called *vittoria mutilata* (hijacked victory), blaming it on "the evil brood" of generals and politicians who had "stabbed the nation in the back."

In October 1922, Mussolini marched on Rome with 30,000 supporters after his paramilitary forces had already grabbed power in most of the cities of the Po Valley. Supported by the military, the business community, and a wide segment of the middle classes—and badly advised—King Vittorio Emanuele rejected the government's demand that he call out the army to suppress the Fascists. Instead he handed power over to Mussolini. In June 1924, Mussolini used the assassination of the anti-Fascist writer Giacomo Matteotti, probably carried out by Il Duce's own henchmen, as a pretext for establishing a dictatorship. By fostering the myth that Italy was somehow robbed of its due, Mussolini and other politicians on the Right laid the foundations for revisionism and Italian cooperation with Nazi Germany in the 1930s.

In the better world the world does not go to war, and Italy does not receive its *irredenta*—territory claimed by Italy—as it is far too weak to challenge Austria by itself, let alone Austria and its German ally. Neither France nor Britain comes to Italy's aid, as both are eager to preserve the peace. The Italian political culture and system continues to be unresponsive to the country's needs. Its bureaucracy is inefficient and corrupt, and its military is poorly trained and led by aristocrats who are more interested in their uniforms, social life, and status than professional training and war plans. No elected government is capable of responding to Italy's economic and financial needs or mediating the growing conflicts between north and south, industrialists and workers, and church and state. So even in counterfactual world an authoritarian regime emerges in a coup engineered by the ever-industrious and power-hungry Benito Mussolini—or someone like him.

In the historical world Spain suffered a military coup in the 1930s, followed by a civil war that pitted pro-Republican, anticlerical, and largely Socialist forces against the Fascist army and the church. Something similar could easily have happened in Italy with roughly the same constellation of opposing forces. Either side could have emerged the victor after a civil war. Any nonparliamentary outcome would have been a tragedy for Italy but not necessarily for Europe, as there would have been no Hitler or indeed any kind of revanchist regime in western Europe with whom an Italian dictator could have allied. In the historical world Nazi Germany and the Soviet Union supported opposite sides in the Spanish Civil War. In the better world, neither exists, and it is accordingly unlikely that a Spanish or Italian civil war would have been internationalized. Their outcome would accordingly be more unpredictable. In the better world these conflicts are avoided, although southern Europe remains deeply divided for some time. Only later in the century does economic progress begin to ease these tensions. Before that, southern Europe sees the occasional coup or coup attempt, and democracy has at best a tenuous hold.

In any of these counterfactual scenarios Europe remains the political and economic center of the world but faces increasingly stiff economic competition from the United States and Japan. In response the Continent develops various forms of supranational cooperation, with Germany taking the lead. Just as everyone learns English today, in the better world most continental Europeans have similar incentives to learn German. Economic integration is facilitated by nearly universal knowledge of German by the region's political, business, and intellectual elites.

The 1915 disarmament conference at the Hague—which never met in the real world because of World War I—makes some progress in regulating land warfare and lays the foundation for the Court of Arbitral Justice. It joins a growing patchwork of international organizations that exercise varying degrees of coordination or control of international postal services, telegraph and communications, shipping, aviation, public health, weights and measures, and trade and investment. Periodic calls were made for a general international organization. In 1918 US President Woodrow Wilson proposed a League of Nations. His initiative was not greeted with enthusiasm by the major European powers, which feared the league would provide a forum for anticolonial movements. Less powerful states worried that it would be an institution exploited by the great powers to impose their preferences on everyone else.

In the better world a League of Nations finally comes into being in 1947, and almost every independent country joins. It has a secretary general, an executive, and a general assembly. The secretary general and executive coordinate the operations of diverse international organizations and any initiatives authorized by the general assembly. Other international institutions develop independently, including the Ascona Seven. Named for the Swiss lake resort where it first convened, it periodically brings together the leaders and representatives of the seven great powers—Britain, France, Germany, Austria-Hungary, Italy (by courtesy), the United States, and Japan. It has its own secretariat, as it periodically sponsors largely economic initiatives, but on several occasions it mediates conflicts or pressures one or both sides to come to the bargaining table. It also manages the great power condominium in the Holy Land. Less powerful countries in the league are nearly unanimous in their view that the Ascona Seven should be made part of that organization and its initiatives subject to the approval of the general assembly. Proposals to this effect are repeatedly stonewalled by the great powers.

As the twentieth century comes to an end, the five great regional power blocs are Europe, Russia, the British Empire, the United States, and Japan. Russia has rapidly developed as the result of a revolution, regime change, and extensive French and German investment. China is wracked by civil war but was not invaded by Japan, whose imperialism is constrained by the other colonial powers. There are tensions among the powers—most notably involving their competing economic interests in China—but leaders and public opinion alike are keen to maintain the peace from which all parties gain. War between or among the great powers, while not unthinkable, is regarded as a remote possibility at best.

Free trade agreements, international investments, trade, and co-production have brought about an increasingly tight-knit developed world. In many ways it resembles our world but with some key differences. For better and worse English is not the world's lingua franca; it must compete with French, German, Spanish, and Japanese. This gives joy to the Québecois but otherwise acts as a barrier to commerce, technological development, and the exchange of ideas. Business executives, professors, and many other professionals must be bi- or trilingual. Multilingualism gives a decided edge to continental Europeans and works against the largely monolingual United Kingdom and United States. It nevertheless makes the United States more cosmopolitan as more Americans, especially in medicine and the sciences, feel the need to study abroad and master the necessary languages.

In the historical world, the United States became a world power, then a superpower, by virtue of its size, population, economic and technological development, and decisive roles in both world wars. Before 1914 the United States was a debtor nation, but by 1918 it had become the largest creditor nation. At the end of World War II the United States

accounted for almost half the world's agricultural and industrial production, and the dollar replaced sterling as the world's principal reserve
currency. The US monopoly on nuclear weapons, which lasted until
1949, made it the world's leading military power. Without two world
wars, the United States is the single most powerful nation by virtue of
its economic and technological development. But it is not a superpower.

In our counterfactual world Europe remains politically, economically, and culturally vibrant. In response to stiff competition from the
United States, the British Commonwealth, and Japan, Europe develops
various forms of cooperation. This is facilitated by widespread knowledge of French and German, the latter the principal language of the region's political, business, and scientific elites. Germany is an economic
and a technological powerhouse and has profited enormously from its
investment and influence in eastern Europe. Its political culture has
evolved, making it less authoritarian and more democratic. In size and
population it cannot compete with the United States, but a unified Europe could. This is not in the cards, as all European states remain committed to their independence and are wary of domination by Germany.

Britain and its empire remain outside the nascent European project. With some success London attempts to mediate among blocs, as it
has cordial relations with all of them. The British Empire is the largest political organization in area and population but is highly decen-
tralized; its richest components have achieved dominion status. It is
economically strong because it has not gone bankrupt in two world
wars. Sterling, along with dollars and the German mark, are the world's
principal currencies.

The Balkans were the flashpoint for war in 1914 and the location of
earlier wars in 1911–13. These states remain deeply divided because of
nationalism and the intermingling of many of the region's nationalities.

Periodic violence erupts, with truces negotiated by Berlin, Vienna, and St. Petersburg, sometimes acting collectively as the Ascona Seven, to keep the region as tranquil as possible to forestall any uprising by their restive nationalities. In 1917, in response to the threat posed to Austro-Russian relations by an aggressive Serbia, Emperor Franz Ferdinand negotiated an understanding with St. Petersburg that delineated spheres of influence for the two empires in the Balkans. Austro-Russian relations became amicable once again, as they had been before Austria's unilateral annexation of Bosnia-Herzegovina in 1908.

In the historical world Balkan unrest was greatly exacerbated by the Ottoman Empire's decline. Often referred to as "the sick man of Europe," the Ottoman Empire lost control of North Africa, and the Italian invasion of Tripoli in 1912 provided the opportunity for Balkan Christians to wage a successful war of liberation. It then touched off a follow-on war among the several Balkan states over the territorial spoils. Bulgaria attacked Serbia and Greece, and Romania joined the war against Bulgaria, which allowed the Ottomans to intervene and regain some lost territory. The 1908 coup against the sultan brought to power a regime of modernizing reformers known as the Young Turks. Reforms were put on hold as the Ottomans entered World War I on the side of Germany and Austria. Fighting in the Caucasus prompted the evacuation of Armenians and the genocide of 1916–17. In 1918 the Ottoman Empire collapsed, and Turkey, its rump successor state, led a war of national unification under the capable leadership of Kemal Ataturk. Greece, supported by Britain, was the principal loser, and the Greek population along Anatolia's coast was either murdered or expelled.

Most of these horrors are avoided in our benign world. The Balkan Wars are followed by an uneasy standoff among Turkey, Bulgaria, and Greece. The Ottoman Empire survives another decade and undergoes rapid modernization under the leadership of Kemal Ataturk, who pushes his secularist and modernist agenda and receives major loans from Britain and Germany. Arab nationalism cannot effectively be suppressed and leads to escalating violence throughout the Middle East. The great powers negotiate the independence of several Arab states and sweetheart deals that guarantee the great powers access to the region's oil. Claiming that no one nationality should control the Holy Land, they collectively establish a protectorate over it. Jews and Arabs alike resent this new manifestation of colonialism, but they are too divided to constitute an effective opposition.

Later in the century European powers confront and resist growing demands for independence in Africa and Asia. Decolonization poses a serious political and military challenge that divides European public opinion. In Britain this problem in fact arose in the context of Ireland, where impending Home Rule threatened a civil war in Northern Ireland that was only forestalled by World War I. Following that conflict, Irish Protestants fought to retain power in the six northern counties in Ireland, while nationalists launched a rebellion against Britain with the goal of independence. Ireland was partitioned in 1921, which triggered an even bloodier struggle within the Irish Republican Army (IRA) between those who accepted partition and de facto independence and those committed to fighting on for de jure independence of a unified Ireland.

Had war been avoided in 1914, the Irish problem would have played itself out in a manner not dissimilar to what happened between 1918 and 1921. Opposition in Britain to the war in Ireland was significant, and the Lloyd George government accordingly made use of mercenary troops—the infamous Black and Tans—in lieu of the regular army. Next up was India, where Tories and Labour alike would have attempted to hold on to this linchpin of empire. In light of the Irish experience, there would have been—and in fact was—a backlash against government repression of nonviolent protesters in India. Indian independence in 1947 was hastened by World War II, which impoverished Britain and strengthened India and its claim to self-governance because of the major buildup of the Indian army and its commendable performance.

Decolonization and the partitions that accompanied it constituted the second major threat to world peace in the historical world. Some colonies were broken up into two or even multiple countries because of intense ethnic or religious conflicts. Antagonisms were further complicated by postindependence territorial disputes. Whenever colonial powers or the United Nations divided territory among rival claimants, fighting invariably broke out after independence.

The British Empire spawned the largest number of partitioned countries: Republic of Ireland/Northern Ireland, Greek and Turkish Cyprus, Israel-Palestine, India-Pakistan, and later Pakistan-Bangladesh. Partition generated some of the world's most intractable problems and accounts for almost one-third (ten of thirty-one) of the post-1945 wars. Partition has also been responsible for a significant percentage of the world's internal violence.

Without two world wars, constructing an alternative future for the Indian subcontinent is relatively easy. During the first decades of the twentieth century, Indian intellectuals favor change but do not seek independence. They want to be treated as loyal citizens of His Majesty's Empire, with access to the rights embedded in all the liberal ideas they have picked up, not just at Oxford and Cambridge but at the many missionary and other schools that have sprung up all over India. Had the British been prepared to go far enough, much of the still-Anglophile nationalist movement could have been co-opted. India could not have

been kept a colony for the long term, but something like dominion status could have evolved along the lines of Canada, Australia, New Zealand, and South Africa. In this scenario independence comes without
partition, and the Indian subcontinent avoids the costly sectarian violence associated with the birth of India and Pakistan—and their subsequent violent rivalry.

France also faces a decolonization crisis. In the aftermath of World
War II Paris struggled to reimpose colonial rule in Indochina, suppressed a rebellion in Madagascar, and in the late 1950s and early 1960s
fought an unsuccessful war to maintain authority in Algeria. French
domestic politics would have evolved differently without the two world
wars, German occupation, and Vichy regime in southern France. There
are nevertheless good reasons for thinking that French governments
would have been equally adamant about maintaining their empire.
The Communists opposed colonialism but only halfheartedly, and
they would have been a much weaker political force in France and Italy
without World War II, resistance movements, and the emergence of the
Soviet Union as a superpower. France could have fought rearguard actions in Indochina, Madagascar, and Algeria, as it did in the historical
world.

Only one conflict arising from partition has been resolved: Sin-
gapore separated from Malaysia in 1965, a division that allowed both
countries to prosper and develop largely cordial relations. Progress has
also been made in Ireland but only after two civil wars and periodic
eruptions of violence. Cyprus, the Middle East, and the Indian subcontinent remain flash points. With the collapse of the Soviet Union,
new partitions have been imposed, and dissatisfied ethnic groups have
pursued separation by violent means from Russia (e.g., Chechnya)
or a successor state (e.g., South Ossetia from Georgia). The breakup

of Yugoslavia, which followed the dissolution of the Soviet Union, spawned another series of violent ethnic conflicts.

The partitions associated with the breakup of the British Empire and the nationality conflicts exacerbated by the dissolution of the Austro-Hungarian, Russian, and Ottoman Empires were particularly violent because they involved large territories, as in the case of the Indian subcontinent, or important strategic or economic locations, as in eastern Europe and the Middle East. During the Cold War some of these conflicts drew in great powers on opposing sides, especially the Middle East, where the United States supported Israel and the Soviet Union, Syria and Egypt.

Could these conflicts have been avoided in the absence of World War I? Some certainly would have been postponed because decolonization would have come later and without the catalysts provided by two world wars. Ireland, in contrast, would have broken up earlier and perhaps more violently. Most important, as I have shown, different British leadership would have avoided the partition of the Indian subcontinent. Nevertheless, considerable ethnic conflict flares within India, and postindependence governments struggle to control or reduce it.

The other major hot spot of postcolonial warfare is the Middle East. In the historical world this is in part attributable to the partition of Palestine and the creation of the successor states of Israel and Jordan. Without World War I there would have been no Balfour Declaration and British Mandate over Palestine. With no World War II the Holocaust would not have happened, and Jewish immigration to Palestine in the 1930s and 1940s would have been much less. Nor would there have been a United Nations to authorize partition and the subsequent creation of the state of Israel in 1947. I say probably because another route to Israel did exist. Nationalism in eastern Europe exacerbated anti-Semitism and hostility toward minorities. Such hostility increased in the aftermath of independence, and the 1920s and 1930s witnessed an exodus of Jews from the region well before the Nazi threat arose. That exodus would have been larger still if Ukraine and Belarus had achieved their independence, which they might have in the absence of a Soviet Union. In the ethnic cleansing, civil wars, and perhaps localized interstate wars that would have accompanied independence, violence and pogroms against Jews would have increased markedly, as they did during the Russian civil war. In this circumstance many Jews would have sought refuge in western Europe or Palestine, and without the Holocaust six million more Jews would have been living in Europe.

The growing size of the Yishuv (the Jewish settlement in Palestine) leads to violent clashes with increasingly numerous Arab nationalists, as it did historically in the 1920s and 1930s. The British mediated between the two sides, although the British generally sided with the Arabs, and quite openly so in the run up to independence. With no British mandate in Palestine—a product of World War I—the Ottomans, or their Turkish successors, would have retained authority in the region and would not have allowed the creation of either a Jewish or an Arab state. Ottoman rulers might nevertheless have regarded the Jews as a useful counterweight to the Arabs and encouraged, or at least not opposed, Jewish immigration.

A more likely scenario is that the Ottomans or their successors lose a series of wars to local nationalist movements, as they had a generation earlier in the Balkans. Ethnic conflict and local wars could have discouraged Jewish relocation from Europe, but many Jews would have had no other recourse with western Europe and the United States increasingly closed to them. A growing Jewish presence would have provoked a violent conflict with Palestinians. Israel's war of independence in 1947–48 was a close thing, and Israel triumphed in part because Jews, their backs against the wall, recognized there was no palatable alternative to victory. Had they lost, they believed they would have been eliminated. Israel also received political backing from the United States and the Soviet Union, and money and arms from Jews in the West, primarily American Jews. Without this support the outcome of a Jewish-Arab war is less certain, although other factors worked in favor of success. The British would have had neither the position nor the incentive to train, arm, and lead the Jordanian Legion, the principal military threat to Israel. With Egypt still in British hands, invasion from the south would not have been possible. London might have had incentive to support the Jews as a counterweight to Arab nationalism, as Britain and France did in 1956.

In this scenario Israel gains its independence with Britain as an ally and many supporters in the United States. In the best scenario Arab-Israeli tensions might have been moderated. The clashing nationalisms of Jews and Palestinians need not necessarily have drawn in other Arabs, who would have been consumed by their own local struggles. If so, the Israel-Palestinian problem would not have become connected to oil the way it did, opening the prospect of a different configuration of political and economic forces in the Middle East.

Still another possibility is concerted action by the major European powers to manage the collapse of the Ottoman Empire. The great powers had a mixed historical record in doing this in Europe, where their rivalries stood in the way. Even coordinated diplomacy was not always effective. A démarche of the great powers had failed to restrain prewar Ottoman violence against Armenians, and we have little reason to think that diplomacy alone would have succeeded elsewhere in the Middle East. In this circumstance a European condominium over the

Holy Land would have been a tempting option for the great powers. Local peoples would have deeply resented such an arrangement, but it would have prevented the bloodshed associated with state formation and independence.

Historically the principal victims of the Ottoman collapse and rising Turkish nationalism were Armenians and Greeks. Both were ethnically cleansed, and the Armenians were victims of genocide. The fate of the Greeks was made worse by their uprising, unwisely backed by Britain. The forces of Kemal Ataturk crushed the Greeks and expelled them from areas along the Anatolian coast that their ancestors had colonized in the seventh century BCE. The persecution of the Armenians was a prewar phenomenon, made much worse during the war when the military junta running the Ottoman Empire feared for its survival. Without the war this genocide could have been avoided.

The political development of the Middle East is of course interesting in its own right. Even the worst-case scenario—the breakup of the Ottoman Empire as the result of bloody wars of succession and subsequent ethnic cleansing and fighting by successor states—would not have provoked a European war. States would have competed for influence, especially in oil-rich regions, but this could have been managed diplomatically as competition for access to oil was in the post-1945 period and today. In the best case the region settles down after the inevitable turmoil and conflict associated with the Ottomans. The region avoids the further colonization that followed World War I but becomes open to Western investment and trade. In these conditions most Arab lands avoid kleptocratic dictators—kleptocrats are bureaucrats out to enrich themselves at others' expense—like Hosni Mubarak, Hafiz and Bashar al-Assad, and Muammar Gadhafi and develop more along the lines of pre-1967 Lebanon. Without Arab-Israeli wars and some degree of prosperity in the region, Islamic fundamentalism has relatively little appeal.

THE PRICE OF PEACE

Every upside has its downside, and this is true of the better world and indeed of any world we can construct. World Wars I and II were responsible for many beneficial innovations and practices that either would not have come about or would have happened at a later date. Recognition of this truth in no way implies that these wars can in any way be considered worth their cost. They gave rise to barbarity and destruction from which the human race has still not fully recovered.

The two world wars had profound long-term political, economic, medical, social, and cultural consequences. Which ones were beneficial is not always obvious as the answer may depend on one's class or beliefs. I will nevertheless offer an assessment of several of these developments, and I will do so by asking what our world would have been like without them. This is, of course, a speculative enterprise because these developments and others interacted in complex ways to bring about their results. Different nonlinear interactions would occur in my alternative world.

Let us begin with economic developments. As I have noted, World War I short-circuited globalization; international trade and investment did not reach the same level until late in the twentieth century. I have argued that uninterrupted globalization would have created strong incentives for peace among the leading powers. The two world wars brought about other kinds of economic changes. They compelled all combatants to exercise far greater state control of the production and distribution of goods, regulation of labor, and distribution of food. In the Soviet Union this was the norm. In Germany, with its more corporate structure and closer working relationship between government and industry, this was more a change in degree than in kind. In Britain and the United States, where laissez-faire capitalism was deeply entrenched in ideology and practice, government supervision of industry and labor, price controls and rationing were radical and largely unpalatable measures. This was also true of military conscription, another practice that had long been routine on the continent.

After both wars, economic and political life reverted to prewar practices only in part. In the United States, where "Return to Normalcy" became the slogan of Warren G. Harding's successful 1920 presidential campaign, much of the country tried hard to turn its back on the war years. To the extent that Americans thought about the Great War, many learned the wrong lesson. They reasoned that the slick Europeans, who would not repay their war debts, had fleeced them and that the "war to end all wars" had only prompted new ones. Americans should accordingly avoid future entanglements. This lesson became the foundation for the policy of isolationism, which severely constrained the Roosevelt administration's ability to respond to the threat of Nazi Germany.

World War I convinced some American business leaders that government intervention was not altogether evil. World War II did much more in this regard because of the greater involvement of the federal government in the economy. Business became much more receptive to government regulation; a 1970 poll revealed that almost 90 percent of the CEOs of Fortune 500 companies favored *more* regulation on the grounds that it created a level playing field from which they expected to benefit. The rise of neoliberalism in the 1980s would bring about a sea change in business attitudes toward government, resurrecting long-discredited and demonstrably false shibboleths about the market's being its own best regulator.

Between the two wars, the United States and the rest of the world suffered through the Great Depression. We will never know whether this event, or something like it, would have happened in the absence of World War I and the extraordinary economic imbalances and disruption it created. Presumably some major recession was unavoidable in a capitalist world economy, and government intervention was essential to alleviating its worst effects and limiting its duration. Franklin Roosevelt's New Deal was helpful in this regard, although wartime industrial production, not the National Recovery Act and related programs, put an end to the Great Depression. The New Deal was tentative in its Keynesian pump priming, but even so it is hard to imagine an American president committed to going this far, or a Congress willing to support his policies, without the experience of successful governmental intervention in the economy during World War I. Roosevelt still met considerable opposition; he was bitterly opposed by the Supreme Court and much of the business community, and the Supreme Court's about-face was a near thing. Some historians maintain that Roosevelt saved capitalism from the capitalists, implying that without the New Deal, economic conditions and unemployment would have been much worse, giving more support to radical political movements on the Right and Left. This is, of course, what happened in Germany and propelled the Nazis to power.

Government intervention was much more pronounced in Britain during both wars and accustomed people in all walks of life to the idea of a partially managed economy. World War I helped to legitimize socialism, and the Labour Party benefited. It supplanted the Liberals at the end of the war and in the next decade would go on to run the government for the first time. World War II paved the way for the welfare state in Britain, a project supported by both major parties, at least in part, in the early postwar period. In Germany economic management was even more centralized during the war, and Hitler's version of the New Deal went much further—and was arguably more effective—in overcoming the Depression.

In the absence of World War I these links among government, industry, and labor never develop, and the American and Britain governments retain their largely unquestioned commitments to laissez-faire economics. In Britain the Liberal Party remains powerful, as its demise owed as much to H. H. Asquith's perceived failure as a war leader. In the United States socialism never gains a toehold; opposition to organized labor remains intense, with the White House consistently siding with big business until the administration of Joseph Kennedy Jr. Labor unions are forced to wage a longer, harder struggle for collective bargaining rights, a struggle that radicalizes the labor movement and damages the economy. Economic growth depends on markets, and American workers were the principal market for American manufacturers. Putting more money in their hands generated more sales and wealth, something business leaders recognize only belatedly.

Without World War I the world's economy still benefits from globalization and, with it, continually improving living standards through the developed world. Prosperity in Europe, even allowing for the occasional recession, strengthens the commitment to peace as people develop materialistic values that are even more pronounced. If arms control had not come about as a way to assist Germany's transition to democracy, the growing sense of security that prosperity and trade encouraged would have prompted efforts to negotiate builddowns of European armed forces. If successful, it would have set in motion a virtuous cycle, making expectations of peace in Europe increasingly self-fulfilling.

The United States is not the economic epicenter of the world but is still the world's largest economy. It profits from a strong Europe, just as it benefits today from a strong Europe and Pacific Rim. The world remains multipolar but without the arms races that threatened the peace in the era before 1914. The United States is not a hegemon, outside its dominant sphere of influence in the Caribbean and Central America. It does not intervene militarily, and certainly not unilaterally, in Asia. Historically US military spending was a smaller percentage of gross domestic product (GDP) than it was for the other great powers and remains so. This pattern changed during the Cold War, when the United States spent more money on its military and foreign military aid than any other state.

At the end of World War II the United States accounted for 46 percent of the world's GDP and today represents a still-impressive 21 percent. Prodigious wealth has allowed the United States to spend an extraordinary percentage of its GDP on its armed forces in comparison with other countries. Fifteen years after the Cold War, the United States still devoted a disproportionate share of its national income to this end. In 2008 it spent 41 percent of its national budget on the military and the cost of past wars, which accounted for almost 50 percent of world defense spending. In absolute terms this was twice the total of Japan, Russia, the United Kingdom, Germany, and China combined. Not surprisingly the United States is the only state with a global military reach.

Military spending and military aid is money wasted in terms of productivity and growth. The spinoffs of military spending are marginal, and the distortion of the economy it promotes is almost entirely negative in its consequences. It sucks up talent in almost every field, keeping it and a significant percentage of the labor force from contributing more productively to the economy. Without hegemony and the military budgets associated with it, the United States is more productive and has a higher standard of living.

The Downside

What about the negative economic consequences of our better world? The Allied blockade of Germany during World War I compelled Germany to develop artificial fertilizer and synthetic foods. The giant German chemical firm I. G. Farben turned to polymer chemistry after the war because of the Allied ban on any kind of fundamental research that could lead to military weapons. DuPont and British companies followed suit out of fear of being left behind. They explored colloids, which led to the development of nylon and other artificial fibers. World War I also accelerated work on blood coagulants that enabled blood transfusions, which became routine by the end of the conflict. World War II promoted massive US and, to a lesser extent, British investment in medical and scientific research. From 1941 to 1945, the United States spent $2 billion on scientific research. The Manhattan Project alone hired almost 20,000 scientists and engineers at 37 locations. Without the two world wars the 1940s do not witness the development of radar, antibiotics, jet engines, artificial rubber, computers, automation, operations research, and of course nuclear weapons. Human needs and capitalist incentives work together to promote radar, raw materials substitutes, and antibiotics, although they all become available at least a decade later than they did historically. So too do jet engines, aluminum fuselages, and advanced avionics, even though the American aircraft industry was seriously competitive, as were their European counterparts.

In our better world economic growth is not as fast in the absence of the GI Bill, which paid for the college and technical education of a generation of World War II veterans and helped many to start businesses.

Without the war the program does not exist. Without the New Deal's commitment to building infrastructure, the country does not benefit from a national program of bridge and road building and rural electrification. After the war no one proposes the interstate highway program, as Republicans—the trucking industry aside—opposed it as a form of creeping socialism. As a result prices of most products are still "slightly higher west of the Rockies," as they were in the historical world well into the 1950s. The Pacific coast also sees less migration from elsewhere in the country. California has no freeways, has a less prestigious public university system, and is less hospitable to the computer hardware and software firms so critical to the region's growth and for moving the country into the postindustrial age.

The information revolution is also delayed for technical reasons. Many developments on which it depended were the result of US government funding for basic and applied scientific research. Continuing government support for science was a response to the Cold War and the fear of falling behind the Soviet Union in the aftermath of its unexpected explosion of a nuclear device in 1949 and the launching of Sputnik in 1957. Lacking these strategic and emotional incentives, Congress does not authorize the many billions that went yearly to the scientific community in the historical world. Private enterprise does invest heavily in basic research—although less so now than in the past—but does not take up the slack. Without Hitler neither the United States nor Britain benefits from the influx of European brain power. In the absence of a greatly enhanced talent pool and no significant government spending on basic research, there are fewer scientific discoveries, and technological progress is correspondingly slower.

My former sister-in-law was the first civilian in the United States to be treated successfully for tuberculosis with antibiotics. In the better world she is unlikely to have survived her childhood. Quick and safe travel across and between continents is a more recent development; in my better world it remains for several decades the preserve of the rich. Airport security is, however, a simple matter because the United States has not become the target of foreign or domestic terrorist attacks. The streaming of movies and other programs on one's computer is a fantasy of science fiction. Nor am I writing this book on a laptop, accessing sources and datasets on the web, and zapping draft chapters to colleagues around the world for feedback.

World War I was arguably a greater promoter of social change than the French Revolution. Everywhere on the Continent, the aristocracy lost political power and cultural influence, and in some countries, most notably the Soviet Union, it disappeared as a class. Of equal importance, the war greatly accelerated the expectation of equal treatment by those who had formerly been characterized as the lower orders. Labor movements and Socialist parties articulated their ideas, which led to confrontations of differing magnitude with representatives of the old regime.

This conflict was most pronounced in Russia, where the Bolsheviks triumphed after several years of brutal civil war, imposed their authority over much of the former territory of the Russian Empire, and initiated revolutionary political, economic, and social changes. The conflict was most muted in Britain, where the aristocracy preserved much of its wealth and social position, even if the war hastened the demise of the values on which its authority and wealth rested.

Before 1914 aristocrats dominated the Tory and Liberal parties alike. As a class the British aristocracy had always been more open to change than its European counterparts. Blueblood Brits saw no disgrace in investing in commercial enterprises or admitting newly rich commoners to their ranks so long as they behaved appropriately. The British aristocracy accommodated itself to political change, accepting and even introducing several reform bills in the nineteenth century that extended the franchise and made the elite's political power ever more dependent on the votes of the masses. The sticking point was the Liberal budget of 1909, which included a tax on property, the principal source of wealth for many Tories. After two years of confrontation, a new election, and a threat by the Liberal government to stack the House of Lords with new members who would approve the measure, they reached a compromise. Tensions became acute again during the 1925 general strike, described by many on both sides as open class warfare. The first Labour government, which lasted nine months with Liberal support in 1924, and Labour participation in the Churchill government during World War II (1940–45), did much to mute class conflict. The postwar Labour government (1945–51) nationalized key industries and introduced the welfare state without provoking a national crisis, and the Tories, when they returned to power in 1951 under Churchill, did not undo this legislation.

For better or worse the First World War was a great leveler. It set in motion a series of progressive changes in attitudes and practices that received another big boost during World War II. The two world wars hastened the emergence of a mass consumer society and values sharply at odds with those of the Victorians. Representatives of the old order often blamed the United States or the Jews for these changes and spoke disparagingly about the new materialism, sexual freedom, voting rights for women, loss of religious faith, and lack of interest in, and respect for, elite culture. In the United States the Christian Right still rails against these developments although not against the Jews.

World War I made the United States the world's dominant economic power. During World War II American Lend-Lease aid sustained Britain and aided a struggling Soviet Union. After the fighting the Marshall Plan and US investment helped to rebuild Britain, western Europe, and Japan. With US power developed American values and practices. American power and cultural change reinforced each other. Both developments may have been to some degree inevitable, but in the absence of the two world wars, they emerge more slowly and in muted form. The old order and its values endure into the mid-twentieth century. This would have put a serious damper on social and political change throughout the Western world.

One of the enduring and admirable triumphs of postwar America is its continuing efforts to overcome prejudice and discrimination based on religion, ethnicity, race, gender, and sexual preference. The election of the country's first Roman Catholic president in 1960 and its first president of African descent in 2008 are symbols of the progress made in the postwar era. It is difficult to imagine the election, or even nomination, of John F. Kennedy or Barack Obama in the absence of the two world wars and the social transformation they engendered. In 1914 the United States was racist to its core; lynchings were common, and racial segregation was rigidly enforced in the South and more informally in other parts of the country. Many Americans were openly anti-Catholic and anti-Semitic. The Ku Klux Klan was not alone in identifying Catholics and Jews as enemies. In the early twentieth century Jews were excluded from prominent New York and Chicago clubs, where they had formerly been welcome, and admission of their sons—forget about their daughters—to Ivy League universities became increasingly problematic. Neighborhoods were redlined, and new homeowners were compelled to sign clauses in purchase contracts committing them not to resell to Jews. A small number of Jews—Louis Brandeis, Felix Frankfurter, and Bernard Baruch among them—gained prominence and were accepted so long as they behaved outwardly like white Anglo-Saxon Protestants. Roman Catholics were only marginally better off.

World War I intensified racial tensions in the United States because of the influx of southern blacks into northern, midwestern, and western cities in search of work. Such migration was much greater during the Second World War and prompted violent race riots in northern cities. Segregation was carried abroad and met considerable opposition in Britain, where local authorities and populations generally refused to accept it and were appalled by the racism of their American allies. The armed forces remained segregated until 1948, and African Americans, with few exceptions, were kept in the lowest ranks and assigned the most menial and unpleasant tasks. Asians were not subject to the same legal restrictions, although they were treated roughly the same way. After Pearl Harbor, authorities rounded up Japanese Americans and packed them off to concentration camps, most of them in desolate locations. In theory these roundups were security measures but, as with Germany's treatment of its Jews, were often motivated by whites' desires to rid themselves of competitors and confiscate their property.

In the 1930s some German Jewish refugees described the United States as more anti-Semitic than Germany. The Viennese economist Joseph Schumpeter, who was not Jewish, did his best to hire Jewish refugee scholars, first at Harvard, where he was a professor, and then at other institutions. He met so much resistance that he gave up. Discrimination against Jews continued well into the 1960s, as the author knows from personal experience. In the 1940s and 1950s on two occasions my parents and I were turned away from hotels where we held reservations once the desks clerks identified us as Jewish. One told my father, "Your kind of people would not feel comfortable here." In 1957, when I started exploring university choices, the guidance counselor at my high school, aware of how few Jewish students would gain places at many of the more prestigious universities, worked with Jewish parents to coordinate their children's applications to maximize the chances of admission. Yale, where I went to graduate school in the early 1960s, still had few Jewish faculty members. Their absence was most obvious in anthropology, a discipline in which Jews were significantly overrepresented elsewhere. At Dartmouth, where I am professor emeritus, the postwar situation was worse. Anti-Semitism was rife, and one college president assured an alumnus who complained about all the "Kike faces" he now saw on campus that measures were being taken to reduce Jewish admissions. Dartmouth was founded in 1769 with a commitment from the outset to educate Native Americans. Only nineteen of them graduated from the institution in its first hundred years.

A sea change has occurred in attitudes toward all out-groups but especially toward Catholics and Jews. Brandeis University was established as a secular institution in 1948 in part to provide a first-rate education to smart Jewish students who could not gain admission to the Ivies. It has had to rebrand itself as Harvard, and the other Ivies removed their restrictions on Jews. The postwar era witnessed the gradual spread of tolerance, beginning with acceptance of Catholics and Jews, then African Americans, women, and more recently homosexuals. All these targets of prejudice now have legal guarantees of equal treatment, and the last frontier in this respect is the ongoing and increasingly successful struggle for gay marriage. The practice of racism is, alas, still pronounced. Police are more likely to stop black and Latino drivers and pedestrians and treat them less civilly. African Americans still earn significantly less than their white counterparts, are less likely to finish high school and attend and graduate from college, and die at a younger age.

How much progress would there have been without two world wars? There is no way to answer this question definitely, so let me lay out what I think is a compelling argument. The move toward tolerance in law and practice is a postwar development. Any major social change has multiple and reinforcing causes, and in this instance, the most important was the collective experience of World War II. Nazi Germany was the principal enemy, and the US government sold the war against Germany to the American people as a struggle against a godless, ruthless, and barbaric regime. Just how evil Nazi Germany was did not become fully apparent until its numerous concentration and death camps were liberated and photos of their emaciated prisoners and stacked corpses repeatedly appeared in newspapers and newsreels. The Nuremberg trials provided additional documentation of the Holocaust and Hitler's plans for other hated races.

American anti-Semitism aroused what the psychologist Leon Festinger calls cognitive dissonance. This occurs when elements of the belief system are contradictory or when beliefs and behavior contradict each other. Either way the resulting dissonance generates anxiety, which must be reduced by denying the contradiction or changing one's beliefs or behavior. Studies that demonstrate the link between smoking and cancers encourage some smokers to give up smoking, or at least try to, and others to deny the efficacy of the studies. Tobacco producers of course encouraged the latter response. Smoking is addictive, but anti-Semitism is not, at least for most people. So the easiest way to overcome the anxiety generated by the contradiction between anti-Semitism and the deep-seated belief that Americans are good people and Nazis the epitome of evil was to renounce anti-Semitic beliefs or behavior. World War II facilitated this strategy in another way. Military service brought together people from every religion, ethnic group, and social class, and it not infrequently put them in positions where they depended on one another for their survival. Small groups under stress tend to bond, and ethnic and religious stereotypes are hard to sustain in this context. More generally soldiers, sailors, and airman—and their female counterparts—made friendships across traditional social divides, and many returned home convinced that all those who had honorably performed military service deserved the respect and admiration of other Americans and a fair deal in the postwar world.

These themes were explored and given a boost by prize-winning, box-office hit movies like *The Best Years of Our Lives* (1946) and *Gentleman's Agreement* (1947). The former was prompted by a *Time* magazine article about the difficulties ex-servicemen experienced in their adjustment to postwar civilian life. In its most political scene Fredric March, working as a bank loan manager, goes into a drunken rage when the loan applications of former servicemen, eager to start their own businesses, are consistently rejected on the grounds that they lack sufficient collateral. He explains to other bank officers that they put their collateral up on the front lines and in the skies over Germany. Directed by William Wyler, it stars Fredric March, Myrna Loy, Dana Andrews, Teresa Wright, Hoagy Carmichael, and Harold Russell, a US paratrooper who lost both hands in a military training accident. The movie won seven Academy Awards in 1946 and became the highest-grossing film in the United States and United Kingdom since *Gone with the Wind*.

In *Gentleman's Agreement* Gregory Peck plays a journalist who passes as Jewish to expose anti-Semitism in New York City and the affluent Connecticut suburb of Darien. He learns that the liberal firm for which he works does not hire Jews and that his Jewish secretary has changed her name and kept her identity a secret. He comes to understand that he will not be invited to certain parties or be allowed to book a room in restricted hotels. His son will be jeered in the street. The reporter's anger at the gentlemen's agreement, a quiet conspiracy to exclude Jews from certain jobs, schools, clubs, and neighborhoods, affects even his relationship with his girlfriend. The movie was considered controversial at the time, as was *Crossfire,* released the same year with the same theme. Both films were nominated for a Best Picture Oscar.

I focus on Jews because they and Catholics were the first groups to benefit from the emerging commitment to tolerance. Once this precedent was established, discriminating against other groups became more difficult because of the logical contradictions and greater dissonance this generated. The civil rights movement met extraordinary resistance, to be sure, but undoubtedly benefited from the earlier efforts of Jews and Catholics for acceptance and changing attitudes toward them. Postwar integration of the armed forces and the expansion of higher education, much of it made possible by the GI Bill, also played a large part in changing white attitudes and practices. In the shadow of a largely successful civil rights movement, Asians, Native Americans, women, and homosexuals found it easier to demand and receive equal treatment.

Another product of both wars was a critical component of tolerance: the mass migration north of southern blacks in search of work in war plants. The first major migration took place during World War I and continued into the 1930s. Beginning in 1941, when war production geared up again, an estimated 5 million African Americans moved to the cities of the Northeast, Midwest, and West. Most were urban workers with more education and skills than their rural counterparts. These migrants and their children benefited from educational, occupational, and social opportunities that were simply unavailable in the Old South. The greater wealth, education, social sophistication, and confidence of the black population made it possible to upgrade and sustain a denser network of black educational institutions. The black professional and business classes these institutions helped to produce provided leadership for the civil rights movement. Thurgood Marshall became chief counsel for the NAACP, participated in many key legal challenges to segregation, and was appointed US solicitor general and then associate justice of the Supreme Court. He did his undergraduate work at Lincoln University and law school at Howard University, where he graduated first in his class after being denied admission to the University of Maryland because of his race.

The famous 1954 US Supreme Court decision in *Brown v. Board of Education* declared school segregation unconstitutional. It was a great victory for the civil rights movement but initially a pyrrhic one as the Court did not insist on enforcement; this was the compromise necessary to secure a unanimous vote. The Eisenhower administration did not want to alienate voters and ignored the problem of school segregation until Governor Orville Faubus mobilized the Arkansas National Guard to prevent blacks from attending the state university in 1958. Eisenhower worried that all the ensuing publicity would hand a major propaganda victory to the Soviet Union. He nationalized the Arkansas militia and used it to force integration of the university. His intervention, and the earlier Supreme Court decision, set a precedent for government support of civil rights at the national level.

Liberals like Thomas Friedman, the economist and *New York Times* columnist, insist that capitalism makes racial, ethnic, and religious tolerance inevitable in the long run. Even if we accept their claim—which

I do not—it says nothing about the pace of change, which likely would have been much slower in my counterfactual world. Instead of being in the forefront of the human rights movement, the United States might have remained a relative backwater until pushed by others to address its racial problems. Who those others might have been is not clear, as the United States was far and away the most powerful and influential country in the postwar era. Other countries that became more tolerant often did so in response to the example set by America. In 1969, I attended the first civil rights demonstration in Northern Ireland, where Catholics staged a sit-in at a public housing complex from which they were excluded. When the protesters did not quite know what they should do next, somebody started singing "We Shall Overcome." Almost everyone knew the lyrics and joined in.

South Africa ended apartheid in response to outside pressure, an increasingly effective economic boycott. Racism was arguably as deeply entrenched as in the United States—its north and south—and there was little practical difference between segregation in the American South and apartheid in South Africa. Northern American whites also expressed considerable opposition to integration on ideological and economic grounds. Race riots in the 1940s revealed that many trade unionists feared competition for their jobs and prospects for advancement. Some businesses were happy to have an inexpensive source of labor. It took an extraordinary change in belief, much organizing and sacrifice by African Americans and their allies, televised footage of African American women and children set upon by dogs and fire hoses, and extensive intervention by the courts, executive branch, and Congress to bring about what can only be described as a revolutionary transformation. Without government intervention, so anathema to conservatives and neoliberals, this would not have occurred. And such intervention would not have occurred without the change brought about by the two world wars.

Our better world is one in which universities nevertheless retain quota systems to limit the number of Jewish students, and the majority of African Americans continue to live in the South in abject poverty. Those with skills and education still earn much less than their white counterparts and are excluded from more prestigious and higher-paying positions. Baseball becomes integrated two decades later than it did historically, and women, in girdles and slips, are still expected to become homemakers or work in the few professions (e.g., teacher, nurse, librarian, secretary) open to them. Homosexuality remains illegal in most states, as do various kinds of heterosexual sex, and these laws are used selectively to punish people who get out of line. Hollywood and television are flourishing industries but reluctant to address controversial social problems. Movies and sitcoms emphasize traditional values, and married couples are still shown pajama clad and in separate beds. There is no powerful evangelical movement or tea party, but then there would be no need for them because existing practices closely resemble the beliefs of both sectors. Our better world is in many ways a prolonged version of the 1950s.

4
Lives in the Best World

THE LAST WORLD WAR I VETERAN DIED IN 2011, AND THE generation that lived through the war as children has all but passed away, too. Any survivors might well need a large-print edition to tackle this book. So we know about the war second hand, from books, documentaries, or perhaps earlier conversations with veterans. My first wife's great uncle Ben fought in France at St. Mihiel Salient and was proud to have been a doughboy. My father was too young to serve but worked on a five-man team that riveted steel plates together in the Fore River Shipyard in Braintree, Massachusetts. He built destroyers, first for the British and then for the Americans, when they entered the war in April 1917. For my dad the war represented steady employment at good pay—for the first time in his life. He and my mother remember the influenza epidemic that followed and how they slept on the fire escape of the building, as conventional wisdom held that fresh air would help ward off infection.

All these lives would have been different without the war. Ben might not have developed the pride and self-confidence that held him in good stead throughout his life. My father was able to put aside a little money and used it to travel to New York to find himself a job as a commercial artist and move into the middle class. He was a resourceful and talented man, and he might have improved his situation in any case, but doing so would have required some other break and probably would have taken longer. My mother, born in 1906, was four years younger and oblivious to the war; she had no recollections of the era other than the flu epidemic. My parents were affected indirectly by the war in many ways. It hastened the demise of Victorian values, making it possible for my mother to work outside the home in an office and to become something of a flapper. My father benefited from the prosperity of the 1920s, another by-product of the war, just before he and his generation would suffer through the Great Depression.

I was a child in the 1940s, so World War I was a distant event for me. I inherited a few toy soldiers from that war, and their uniforms looked quaint, as did the soldiers themselves, because some paint had chipped off their faces. My uncle Jerry, who served in the Quartermaster's Corps in World War II, gave me his *Boy's Book About the Great War,* which he had received as a gift from his aunt in the early 1920s. Every year I watched the still-large contingent of World War I veterans leading the Memorial Day Parade. Like most people, I had no idea how that event and its aftermath had affected my life. Its indirect effect was decisive because German defeat made possible the rise of Hitler and the advent of the Holocaust.

The penumbra of the Great War falls across all our lives. This shadow may be longer and less defined in many cases, as I can safely assume that most readers are younger than I, born after World War II, members of the Baby Boom or an even more recent generation, and may not be familiar with the individuals whose actions proved to be so consequential.

The cast of characters comes from diverse countries, backgrounds, and professions, in keeping with my contention that changes at the international level trickle down to affect all our lives. How this happens is not necessarily apparent, but the changes in their lives are often profound.

POLITICS

To recap: in my better world the Russians had a revolution, but the Soviet Union did not exist. The Bolshevik coup was made possible by clever rhetoric and good organization. The more fundamental reason was war-weariness. The government of Alexander Kerensky, which replaced the czarist regime in 1917, was committed to keep fighting in World War I on the side of the Allies. Leon Trotsky and V. I. Lenin promised bread and peace, both in short supply after three years of war that claimed 3 million Russian lives. Without this suffering the Bolsheviks would have been much less appealing and the government better able to suppress them. Assuming a revolution and a coup, the Bolsheviks would have been crushed, their principal leader, Trotsky, likely killed in the attempt. Stalin, a mere member of the rank and file at the time, would have fled and gone back to his earlier life in Georgia as a small-time criminal.

Lenin was in exile in Switzerland, where he issued periodic appeals for revolution. In real life he frequented the art nouveau Odeon café, which also attracted Chaim Weizmann, who would become the first president of Israel; the Austrian writer Stefan Zweig; and the exotic dancer Mata Hari. Before the war Benito Mussolini and Albert Einstein came to the Odeon in Zurich to drink coffee, read newspapers, and chat with friends. Mussolini would exchange his socialism for rabid nationalism and go on to become the dictator of Italy for two decades. Weizmann left Zurich in 1904 for Manchester, England, to accept a senior lectureship in chemistry. Lenin would have become increasingly frustrated with his life in Switzerland. He would have emigrated—not to Russia, where he would become persona non grata after the failed coup—but to Paris perhaps—if the French would have him. In the real world, Kerensky, the last leader of the parliamentary regime overthrown by the Bolsheviks, escaped to Paris, then fled to the United States in 1940 when the Germans conquered France. Lenin might have done the same, and imagining that he becomes a professor of Russian history and politics at Columbia University is not difficult. His students have great respect for his knowledge and find riveting his insightful descriptions of the Socialist and other figures he knows. They nevertheless dislike his tendency to award low grades and his inability to tolerate opposing points of view. At some point he writes his memoirs and becomes involved in the local labor movement. His obvious point of entry would have been the Left-oriented International Ladies Garment Workers Union (ILGWU), which employed many Russian speakers.

The ILGWU used traditional means of recruiting members and pressuring employers, but it was also creative on both counts. In 1937 the Labor Stage premiered the union's production of the musical *Pins and Needles* with an entirely amateur cast of union members. The play took potshots at Fascist European dictators and, closer to home, the Daughters of the American Revolution and other retrograde movements. Like cabaret, new skits were introduced to keep the show current.

In this counterfactual world the play would have had slightly different targets, and the remarkably creative Lenin finds a new and satisfying avocation as writer of its most acerbic lyrics.

Next to Russia, the major powers most affected by World War I were Germany and Austria-Hungary. Germany lost significant territory in addition to an estimated 2.4 military and civilian lives. The Austro-Hungarian empire dissolved, leaving Austria and Hungary as two small rump states. The cost in lives to the former empire is estimated at about 1.6 million. France and Britain lost 1.7 and 1 million lives, respectively, but no territory; France increased in size when it regained Alsace-Lorraine from Germany. In the absence of war people from these countries would have led different lives, some of them only marginally different and others very much so. Political and military leaders, and anyone in uniform, are the obvious candidates for the more dramatic changes in trajectory.

The Austrian Adolf Hitler (né Schickelgruber) fought in the German army on the western front, was wounded and decorated, and was promoted to the rank of corporal. After the war he returned to Munich, organized the Nazi Party, and was arrested in November 1923 after the unsuccessful Beer Hall Putsch that he led with the former field marshal Erich Ludendorff. Hitler's later career needs no elaboration, and along with Stalin and Mao, he has the distinction of being one of the three deadliest mass murderers of the twentieth century. In the alternative world Hitler's life is dramatically different because, without a European war, he does not join the army, has no postwar political career, and certainly never becomes Der Führer. He remains a rabid anti-Semite, to be sure, and an unsuccessful artist who must supplement his income by painting houses. His great interest outside politics is alternative medicine, as it was in real life. He sets up a successful mail-order business that sells quack products. People in the cafes he frequents tell him he looks a lot like the famous comic Charlie Chaplin, but he is not amused.

Other Nazi leaders fare no better. Hermann Göring, born in Bavaria in 1893, was an air ace in World War I and head of the Luftwaffe in World War II. He was fascinated by toys at an early age, and during the Boer War, he dressed in a Boer uniform. At sixteen he was sent to a military academy in Berlin, from which he graduated with distinction. In 1912 he joined the Prince Wilhelm Regiment of the Prussian army. With some difficulty he managed to learn to fly and soon distinguished himself as a fighter pilot. His squadron was in awe of his arrogance. In our alternative peaceful world Göring finds military discipline even more confining and spends as much time as possible in the mountains. As a youth he had scaled Mount Blanc and other challenging peaks, and in peacetime he was freer to indulge this passion. Göring's politics were conservative, and he opposed democratization of Germany, but in the absence of a world war and a German defeat, he does not become engaged in extralegal political activities.

Heinrich Himmler, Hitler's minister of the interior and overseer of the Gestapo and the death camps, was, like Hitler, deeply committed to killing Jews. Himmler grew up in a conservative Catholic Bavarian family. When he was in high school, his father, the principal, had Heinrich spy on other pupils and described him as "a born criminal." Himmler was neither athletic nor well-coordinated; he barely made it through military training and served in a reserve regiment in World War I. After the war he studied agronomy and, through his participation in a paramilitary unit, came into contact with Hitler. Himmler embraced Nazi ideology and its anti-Semitism. Himmler had difficulty relating to people and held puritanical views about women, sex, and marriage. Hitler and the Nazis offered him a sense of belonging and power. He was a born follower, drawn to strong personalities. In the better world he became the sycophantic sidekick of a successful businessman-cum-gangster.

Germany's emperor, Kaiser Wilhelm, was another damaged personality. He was physically deformed, having been born with one shriveled arm, which may have accounted in part for his deep sense of inadequacy and inferiority. From an early age he tried to overcompensate by cultivating an image of a decisive and strong-willed man. His favorite mode of dress was the military uniform, of which he owned many. He surrounded himself with military courtiers and occasionally dressed in drag with them. He loved to attend maneuvers and war games on horseback, and the general staff routinely rigged the games so his side would win. He was famous for his blustery rhetoric but had little backbone. At the height of the July 1914 crisis that led to World War I, he had a nervous breakdown and was incommunicado for twenty-four hours in Potsdam. When the German offensive in France stalled at the Marne, Wilhelm sought refuge in delusions. He spent the rest of the war in a fortress outside Coblenz, increasingly disconnected from reality and an object of scorn to the general staff. When the Republic was proclaimed in November 1918, he fled to Holland, where he spent the remaining years of his life.

In our better world Wilhelm never becomes reconciled to his status as a constitutional monarch. He makes inappropriate statements to journalists and proves a great embarrassment to German politicians. European leaders learn to discount his unguarded public remarks. Wilhelm dies in 1940 and is succeeded by his oldest son. Frederick Wilhelm Victor Augustus Ernest is peacefully inclined, although he served in the army during World War I. In 1914 he described that conflict as "undoubtedly . . . the most stupid, senseless and unnecessary war of modern times." From April 1916 on in the historical world he implored the general staff to halt its costly offensive at Verdun because it accomplished nothing beyond mutual slaughter. Frederick Wilhelm marries Duchess Cecelia of Mecklenburg-Schwerin but is reported to have had flings with the American opera singer Geraldine Farrar and dancer-spy Mata Hari. He dabbles in postwar German politics and in the years after World War I sought to return home from Dutch exile.

In the better world, Frederick Wilhelm reigns as kaiser from 1940 to 1951 and is well liked in Germany and abroad. He carefully adheres to his constitutional role and uses his position to build trust and friendships with the remaining royal houses of Europe. Two of his children marry into the British House of Saxe-Coburg and Gotha, which, absent World War I, had not changed its name to Windsor. The German and British royal families continue to intermarry in the next generation. Two sons from these marriages suffer from severe hemophilia, the result of inbreeding among Queen Victoria's descendants.

In Britain the two political figures most affected by the war were David Lloyd George and Winston Churchill. Lloyd George was an enterprising Welsh politician of humble origins who spoke English as a second language. He became prime minister in 1916 as head of the wartime coalition and stayed in office until 1922. Lloyd George played a major role at the Versailles Peace Conference, where he did his best, in alliance with France's Georges Clemenceau, to oppose Woodrow Wilson's plans for a nonpunitive peace. Lloyd George also prosecuted the war in Ireland against the Irish Republican Army and presided over that country's partition in 1921. Before 1914 he was a leading reformer and attempted to tax unearned agricultural income and introduce the graduated income tax. In our alternative world he remains a committed reformer, and the Liberal Party, which he leads, remains a major political party but often allies with Labour to form governments.

Little could have prevented Winston Churchill from having one of the most colorful political careers of the century. In World War I he served as first lord of the admiralty and was one of the sponsors of the disastrous Gallipoli campaign, an amphibious assault on the Dardanelles intended to knock the Ottoman Empire out of the war. This costly failure for the British and Anzac forces seriously damaged Churchill's career. Out of office, Churchill spent some time as a lieutenant colonel on the western front. After the war he held a variety of positions, advocated intervention in the Russian Civil War in the hope of strangling the Bolshevik regime, and spent the 1930s in the political wilderness warning against the growing Nazi threat. He became prime minister in May 1940 and led Britain to victory in World War II.

Churchill was a controversial prewar political figure because of his independence from traditional class interests, willingness to make tough decisions, and change of parties from the Liberals to the Tories. Nobody denied his talent, but many believed he was someone who would not let principles stand in the way of his career. In our better world Churchill also has a long but turbulent political career. He is an unusual Tory in his support for all kinds of programs to benefit the working class while doing everything he can to hold on to the empire. Depending on one's political perspective, he can be classified as a reformer or a reactionary. He becomes colonial secretary and makes consistently disparaging remarks about Mohandas Gandhi—not unlike those he made in real life—and authorizes the use of force against nonviolent Indian protesters. The government replaces him with a blander, more conciliatory, figure, and India gains dominion status. In retrospect some historians argue that Churchill's oppositional role unwittingly hastened this transition. In his best-selling memoir Churchill acknowledges his last-ditch support of colonialism as the biggest blunder of his political career.

France benefits greatly from the extended decades of peace. World War I nearly wiped out a generation of young men and sapped the self-confidence, vigor, and economic and cultural life of the country. In our better world political and economic challenges still periodically stress the Third Republic, and the army and church continue to fight rear-guard actions against their loss of influence. The Republic nevertheless thrives in the absence of World War II, German occupation, and Vichy. Without the Soviet Union and resistance, the Communists are not nearly as popular as they were in post-1945 France. Georges Clemenceau is a distinguished prime minister but known for his defense of civil freedoms, not his prosecution of a war. The greatest French leader of the century is Léon Blum, a moderate leftist who entered politics after the trauma of the Dreyfus Affair in the 1890s, when a French Jewish officer was convicted on trumped-up charges of spying for the Germans and sent to Devil's Island. In the 1930s he became France's first Jewish prime minister and the target of hatred from the army and church. In our better world this opposition is not nearly as strong and the Socialist party is stronger. Blum has the National Assembly pass a series of political and economic reforms that lay the groundwork for rapid industrial development and ultimately better relations between labor and management.

Charles de Gaulle is a little-known but creative cavalry officer who develops an advanced doctrine of tank warfare. It never progresses beyond the drawing board because the army is controlled, like its British and German counterparts, by largely incompetent aristocrats who oppose any innovation that threatens the central role of cavalry. In disgust de Gaulle resigns his commission and supports himself by writing books about modern warfare, including a counterfactual novel in which France wins an imaginary war against Germany by virtue of its Blitzkrieg strategy. He meets Winston Churchill at a book convention, where both have come to flog their latest works, and the two men become lifelong friends.

US President Wilson serves two terms and achieves renown as a reformer, tackling several issues, some with success, that were put on hold when the United States entered the war in April 1917. In our alternative world he engages in more extensive trust busting, has Congress recognize labor's right to collective bargaining, and expands the national park system. He resists all suggestions that he do something to improve the status of African Americans and remains a lifelong supporter of Jim Crow. Wilson still suffers a stroke.

Franklin Roosevelt, arguably the country's greatest president, along with Washington and Lincoln, still gets elected to office. Although the country faces periodic recessions, it does not suffer the Great Depression, and Roosevelt, like Churchill, is someone whose policies transcend his class interests. Influenced by his cousin Teddy and his wife Eleanor, and the Democratic machine in New York State, FDR becomes, as in real life, increasingly liberal on labor and agricultural issues. He serves two unremarkable terms as president, building on and extending the Wilsonian reform program.

Five consecutive terms of Democratic presidents convince voters that change is desirable. The GOP standard-bearer, Governor Thomas Dewey of New York, wins the White House in 1944. He is a particularly appealing candidate because of the spate of scandals that engulfed the last Democratic administration and his success as district attorney in prosecuting gangsters and corruption in New York. A representative of the so-called eastern establishment, he does not undo any of the major Democratic reforms but pursues more conservative fiscal policies, sides with business against unions, and takes more interest in foreign affairs. He pushes for wider use of the death penalty, as he had as governor, and sponsors bills that increase federal support for all levels of education. He occasionally graces White House parties and public events with his fine singing voice. Liberal cartoonists frequently depict him as a groom atop a wedding cake because he has the same immobile, characterless good looks and is always impeccably dressed.

After Dewey's two terms in office the political pendulum swings back to the Democrats, and Americans elect their first Catholic president, Joseph Patrick Kennedy Jr. Born in 1915, Joe was the oldest son of a wealthy Irish immigrant turned whiskey importer and ambassador to the Court of St. James. Educated at Harvard and the London School of Economics (LSE), JPK was groomed for the presidency. In the historical world, Joe was a pilot and was shot down over the English Channel in August 1944. In our counterfactual world there is no World War II and he survives and prospers. He is a virile, intelligent, and well-spoken man who nicely integrates the grace and humor of his Irish Catholic background with cosmopolitanism and intellectual sophistication derived from his elite education. He hones his political skills through handshaking, baby-kissing campaigns, and hard backroom bargaining. Like most of his family, he is an avid smoker of Cuban cigars. He is a delegate to the 1940 Democratic convention and is elected to Congress in 1942 and to the Senate in 1950. Unlike his father, a conservative Democrat, Joe has been influenced by his Socialist mentor at the LSE, Harold Laski, and allies himself with the labor movement. Joe is a strong supporter of civil rights but quiet about it because he has national political ambitions.

Elected president in 1960, Joe quickly integrates the armed services and introduces legislation to recognize the civil rights of all minorities. Congress approves a watered-down and almost meaningless law after southern Democrats filibuster to prevent the passage of anything threatening to them and their constituents. Joe's younger brother John (Jack) serves as attorney general and is not at all aggressive in enforcing civil rights or particularly responsive to pleas from southern activists for federal protection. After several murders of civil rights workers in Mississippi, a third Kennedy brother, Robert (Bobby), who is Jack's assistant and otherwise pursuing crime bosses, convinces his brother to have the FBI become more engaged.

Joe is most successful in addressing labor-management issues. Trade unions confronted eight years of a hostile Republican administration and now make considerable progress in organizing. Their efforts lead to head-on clashes with the major auto companies, especially Ford, whose labor practices are downright reactionary. The president convinces Ford's management to make reasonable concessions to labor, threatening to take lucrative government contracts elsewhere if they do not. Ford boss Robert McNamara understands that he has no choice but to concede. Several of the autoworkers' successful demands concern workplace safety; the worker injury rate at Ford's plants is truly appalling. President Kennedy convinces Congress to create a new cabinet-level agency to oversee worker safety nationally and to give it adequate enforcement authority.

JPK faces an equally serious confrontation on the domestic front. In 1944 he married Athalia Fetter, a former model and Broadway showgirl. Many Americans were more familiar with her than her husband because she had hosted the radio, and later television, game show, *Winner Take All.* JPK has found life with Athalia to be less than soothing since his unsuccessful run for the Democratic presidential nomination in 1956. Joe's political advisers had urged him to make Athalia give up her career and become a full-time housewife and mother to their two young daughters. Her sex appeal, independence, and obvious lack of interest in being a homemaker will not sit well with either convention delegates or voters. She reluctantly agreed but once in the White House became an even more activist first lady than Eleanor Roosevelt.

Athalia's outspoken support for civil rights for women has produced a storm of bad publicity and a precipitous drop in the polls for Joe. He is compelled to rein her in, if only to demonstrate to voters that he wears the pants in the family. The president and his wife are at each other's throats in private while pretending to be a fairy-tale couple in public. Joe suggests that Athalia direct her energy to redecorating the White House, a suggestion that only infuriates her. In an unguarded moment she tells him he should have married Jackie, his brother's wife, as she is a vacuous socialite who would love nothing more than basking in the publicity of being the first lady. Jack is another source of trouble as his sexual escapades become more blatant. Reporters drop their boys-will-be-boys wall of silence after a paparazzo in a small plane buzzes Jack's sailboat and snaps a picture of him in a compromising position with the well-endowed moll of a Mafia boss whom Bobby has been trying to indict. Jack is forced to make a public apology, but his extramarital activities continue.

In the 1950s Negro activists adopted Gandhi's strategy of nonviolent protests against discrimination but with little effect. Local political authorities in the South and North arrest and imprison ringleaders with the open support of the Republican administration and tacit backing of many trade unions. Renewed protests in the 1960s, led by prominent southern Baptist ministers and northern professionals and students, elicit more support but fail to remove key legal barriers or make much progress in changing social attitudes. The armed forces slowly become integrated in the 1960s, as do some Ivy League and avant-garde universities. Much to the annoyance of her husband, Athalia uses her own resources to establish a scholarship at Harvard for a southern Negro student. She is already something of a flash point for those opposed to greater freedom for women and Negroes. While attending a ceremony in New York City, she is attacked by a crazed knife-wielding assailant and badly wounded. She becomes even more outspoken after her recovery and a symbol for the emerging women's movement.

The Cleveland Indians, keen to improve their pennant chances, hire young Curt Flood in 1962. He consistently bats better than .300 in a long career and paves the way for other Negro players. Flood is an articulate and sophisticated man who becomes more outspoken as the color barrier comes down in baseball. He defies white stereotypes of blacks—as Negroes now insist on being called—which invokes the ire of racists everywhere. It also prompts more open-minded whites to rethink their views about race, as does the rhetoric and obvious intelligence of black civil rights leaders. Flood famously tells a television talk show host that he is "proud of the black skin God gave me but only wish he had made it thicker." The cry of "Thicker Skin!" becomes a rallying call for civil rights activists facing fire hoses, police batons, and police dogs as the nonviolent protests escalate.

Many white liberals, including the aged Eleanor Roosevelt, support the black activists. She becomes a martyr for the cause when she dies from a stroke after being arrested in Mississippi. Country singer Elvis Presley divides his fans by marching alongside Little Richard and Harry Belafonte in the same civil rights action. Interviewed after his release from jail, Presley tells reporters that god created all people equal and this is how they should be treated.

THE ARTS

Before 1914 Western culture was centered in Paris, London, Berlin, and Vienna. After 1945 the locus shifted to New York. In our better world European cities remain vibrant cultural meccas and, as in the case of jazz, draw many Americans to Europe. This difference has important implications for race relations.

Within the United States racial stereotypes break down as more whites interact with blacks and more blacks achieve success in business, the professions, performing arts, and film. This happens more slowly than in the historical world. As their acceptance grows, black performers leave Stepin Fetchit and minstrel roles behind for sophisticated comedic and dramatic roles. Americans witness their first interracial kiss on screen in an imported French film that provokes a public debate. Miscegenation laws remain on the books in many states well into the 1970s. Europe fosters racial tolerance in another important way. Jazz is a musical form whose primary appeal is within the black community. It finally breaches the race barrier in a big way because of the acceptance it wins on the Continent. First the blues and then swing take Europe by storm in the 1930s and 1940s. Louis Armstrong has been a cultural hero in France since the 1920s. During the next decades many American jazz musicians migrate to England, France, and Germany, where they find good-paying jobs as patrons jam clubs to see and hear them. White American musicians follow to learn the new and evolving music first hand from its black pioneers. Mixed ensembles of black and white American and European jazz musicians become increasingly common, although such collegiality is still outlawed in much of the United States.

Jazz, originally based in New Orleans, was a blend of African and European musical traditions. Early forms of the blues built on the call-and-response tradition of southern Negro churches but also emphasized innovation. In New Orleans and Dixieland jazz soloists were encouraged to riff on melodies while rhythm sections "comped" them by playing appropriate chords and rhythms. In Europe jazz builds on, some would say integrates, klezmer because so many Jews have taken up the new musical style and jam with its American innovators. Pioneered by Yiddish-speaking Jews from the shtetls of eastern Europe, klezmer is performed by small ensembles and characterized by expressive melodies, reminiscent of the human voice, complete with laughing and weeping. Efforts to mimic the human voice on the clarinet parallel efforts by jazz musicians to do so on this and other instruments. Louis Armstrong, who in the historical world had been all but adopted by a Jewish family when a young boy in New Orleans and always wore a Star of David around his neck, helps to pioneer this synthesis.

Louis Armstrong, Duke Ellington, Billie Holiday, Benny Goodman, Glenn Miller, Charlie "Bird" Parker, and Miles Davis lead different lives in this better world. Armstrong spends most of his career in Europe, making only occasional visits to the United States. Duke Ellington sees little hope for racial progress in the United States and moves to London and eventually becomes a British citizen. He collaborates from time to time with Cole Porter and produces music for big bands, film scores, and classical ensembles and orchestras. The Russian composer Igor Stravinsky, who lives in Paris, calls Ellington the most creative musical talent of his generation. In 1950 Ellington is knighted, and two years later he shares the Nobel Peace Prize with Louis Armstrong. The Oslo-based prize committee characterizes both musicians as ambassadors of goodwill who have brought the peoples of the world together by bridging diverse musical styles.

Billie Holiday, born in Philadelphia in 1915, leads a miserable life as a child and young girl and spends time in and out of reform school. She is raped and then works as a prostitute turning tricks for $5 in a Harlem bordello. She gradually finds singing jobs in clubs, helps to pioneer swing, and greatly influences the young Benny Goodman and Artie Shaw. She cuts some records with Teddy Wilson and Lester Young, and then in 1938 she begins to sing for Count Basie's band. Basie is booked for an extended European tour, where Holiday and the band are a big hit. She begins an affair with a French musician and remains in Paris when the band returns home because she is violently opposed to segregation in the United States. She cuts records with different bands and rivals Edith Piaf as France's leading torch singer.

Benjamin David (Benny) Goodman, born in Chicago in 1909, grew up in the same kind of poverty as Billie Holiday, although with an intact and loving family. He fell in love with music when exposed to it in the synagogue as a young boy and took free lessons at Hull House. In high school he played clarinet in local bands, where he imitated New Orleans and other jazz styles. Benny and his brother quit school to play professionally. Their father died in an accident in 1926, and in my better world Benny takes off for Europe in search of the real jazz action. He develops a form of swing heavily influenced by klezmer and returns to the United States in 1950 to great acclaim. At home Glenn Miller's band is extremely successful, and Miller, who in this alternate world is not a casualty of World War II, lives a long life. He winds up writing music and performing for the film industry in Hollywood. Arthur Jacob Arshawsky (Artie Shaw), born in New York in 1910, becomes another popular bandleader but seeks to blend jazz and classical music. He ultimately goes solo to indulge his love of innovation.

Jazz does not break out of the ghetto in the United States until the late 1940s and early 1950s. Musicians little known to white audiences—among them Charlie Parker, Thelonius Monk, Dizzy Gillespie, and Miles Davis—must still go to Europe and gain acceptance there before being welcomed into mainstream American culture. In the historical world Harlem, and black urban communities everywhere in the United States, were overwhelmed by heroin after 1945. Many black and white jazz musicians used heroin, which was known as "horse" in the ghetto. Gene Ammons, Chet Baker, Art Blakely, Ray Charles, Al Cohn, John Coltrane, Miles Davis, Stan Getz, Dexter Gordon, Billie Holiday, Hank Mobley, Gerry Mulligan, Lou Levy, Fats Navarro, Anita O'Day, Bud Powell, and Sonny Rollins constitute merely a partial list. Charlie Parker died at thirty-four of heart failure attributable to drugs and drink. Without World War II the United States would have had smaller ghettos, fewer urban gangs to push drugs, and very different social conditions. Harlem might have avoided the drug plague, and at least some of the musicians who succumbed would have been overseas and relatively safe. Many jazz musicians wanted to emulate Bird and falsely believed that heroin would give them the insight and relaxation to play as fast and as creatively. Miles Davis became hooked only when he returned from Paris to confront American racism after being treated as an equal human being in France. If Bird and Davis had avoided heroin, many other jazz musicians would have, too.

At the beginning of the twentieth century, Paris was at the center of artistic life. James Joyce, Georges Braque, Marc Chagall, Amadeo Modigliani, Pablo Picasso, Maurice Vlaminck, Virginia Woolf, Serge Diaghilev, and Igor Stravinsky were all residents. In 1908 Picasso gave a banquet for fellow artist Henri Rousseau, and the guest list included the poet Guillaume Apollinaire, the artists Georges Braque and Maurice Vlaminck, and the writers Gertrude Stein and Alice B. Toklas. On May 18, 1922, at the luxurious Majestic Hotel in the Avenue Kléber in Paris, Proust, Joyce, Picasso, Stravinsky, and Diaghilev met for the only time. They were guests of the British writer Sydney Schiff and his wife, Violet, who wanted to celebrate the premiere of Stravinsky's ballet *Le Renard*, performed by Diaghilev's *Ballets Russes*. In retrospect this gathering was the high point of European modernism.

In the post–World War II era the art world was centered in New York. Marcel Duchamp, Fernand Léger, Wassily Kandinsky, and Piet Mondrian had arrived from Europe. They interacted with a younger generation of Americans that included Jackson Pollock, Willem de Kooning, Helen Frankenthaler, Franz Kline, Robert Motherwell, and a half-dozen others who constituted the New York school of abstract expressionism.

In the better world these artists would have no reason to flee their countries of origin or their adopted home of Paris. Some of the Americans would have gone to Paris and spent at least part of their careers there, as generations of American artists had done before them.

European artists also fare better in the absence of World War I. The Austrian painter Egon Schiele and his pregnant wife died in 1918 of influenza. Egon Schiele was born to German-Czech parents in a small town on the Danube, and after his father died of syphilis, Schiele was raised by his uncle. His uncle recognized Schiele's artistic talent and sent him to Vienna to study. He found the art academy's conservatism repellant and sought out Gustav Klimt, known for his generous mentoring of younger artists. In 1909 Schiele founded the Neukunstgruppe (New Art Group) with other antiestablishment artists. He had a turbulent career, which included being run out of the town of Krumau with his lover for hiring teenage girls as models, legal prosecution for allegedly seducing an underage girl, and a conviction for producing art that was deemed pornographic. To demonstrate his disgust the presiding judge burned one of Schiele's erotic drawings. Schiele married in Vienna and three days later was drafted and assigned to guarding Russian prisoners of war in Prague. He later returned to Vienna, where he held a successful exhibition at the end of the war. His last works were sketches of his wife, who died three days before he did.

In the alternative world Egon and his pregnant wife do not die of influenza as they are better fed and stronger and recover from this virus. Egon becomes the star of the autumn 1918 Secession Exhibition; buyers from all over Europe snap up his paintings. He responds well to fatherhood and begins a series of paintings of his son. They are initially similar to his paintings of adult nudes: contorted, outlined figures composed of pale, sometimes sickly, flesh tones, accented with reds and blues that suggest erotic potential but severe alienation. Gradually his portraits of his son, and to some extent those of other people, become less angular and show more of an inner light, heightening the tension between their human potential and social situation.

Gustav Klimt also died in 1918 of a stroke that followed his struggle with influenza. He too survives and exhibits at the same show. Both artists appeal to the sophisticated collectors in Vienna's Jewish community. In New York Solomon R. Guggenheim is drawn to modern art, Viennese art in particular, and brings both artists to New York to do portraits of his family. He later brings Josef Hoffmann from Vienna to construct a museum on Fifth Avenue to house his secessionist collection and related works. Schiele and Klimt live to 78 and 82, respectively; along with Pablo Picasso, Vassily Kandinsky, Marc Chagall, Schmuel

Katz, and Thomas Upschulte are recognized as the greatest artists of the century.

Katz was born in the Ukraine and killed as a teenager with his family in a pogrom during the Russian Civil War. In our better world the Russians do not have a civil war so pogroms are many fewer, and Katz matures, displays precocious talent, and studies in Vitebsk, in today's Belarus. Vitebsk is home—as it was historically—to one of Russia's two great art schools, led by Marc Chagall, with Kasimir Malevich and El Lissitsky on its faculty. Katz moves on to Vienna and becomes another of the innovative artists for whom Klimt became a mentor. Katz produces collages, some using ordinary objects juxtaposed in bizarre and often unsettling ways. He expands into printing, architecture, and furniture.

Before 1914 Russians actively participated in European art. Kandinsky became part of the Munich Blaue Reiter school. Chagall and Malevich exhibited in Paris, and wealthy Russian collectors bought French art. Futurism, developed by Filippo Marinetti in 1909, was taken up in Russia by Natalya Goncharova and Mikhail Larionov in 1914. Katz continues this tradition and lives in Paris, but he makes frequent visits to Russia and facilitates continuing exchanges between Russian artists and intellectuals and their Western counterparts. Katz becomes a leading figure in Russian suprematism, which develops differently than it did in the historical world because there is no Stalin to suppress its artists and compel them to produce Socialist realism (a crude representational form of art glorifying the achievements of workers and the Russian Revolution). In the absence of the Russian Revolution, suprematism is avant garde but not overtly political. Some of its artists turn to mystical portrayals of the Russian past, as Kandinsky did in the prerevolutionary era. Others embrace modernism, a movement with prominent representatives in St. Petersburg, Munich, Paris, and New York.

Russian suprematism influences, if not inspires, artists associated historically with the Bauhaus movement, which stressed the combination of crafts and construction in simplified forms. So too did the Viennese architects Otto Wagner and Adolf Loos. Wagner built Vienna's underground railway. He emphasized new materials, not only for their value in construction but for their aesthetic qualities, and he made sure that they were highly visible in buildings, bridges, and arches. His structures minimized ornament, and their plainness and directness were intended to reflect modern life. Adolf Loos pioneered an even more revolutionary approach to architecture. Its purpose, he insisted, was to shake people up, as should design, clothing, and ordinary manners, and help liberate them from their enslavement to material culture.

Katz, in contrast, is influenced by the secessionists and the more elaborate Jugendstil architecture, and he develops a form of modern architecture that values playful decoration, variety over uniformity, and curves over lines. His buildings and furniture are intended to make people feel welcome and good about themselves. He is widely emulated in central and eastern Europe, whereas in northern Europe the more severe and angular Bauhaus style dominates. Architecture is another example of the cultural divide that separates these two regions of Europe. In Barcelona, of course, Antoni Gaudí offers another example, as Friedensreich Hundertwasser would later in Vienna.

Unlike Gaudí, Katz is utterly secular and, like many secessionist artists, bohemian in lifestyle. He has a string of affairs with married women, among them Alma Mahler and the wife of a prominent count. The count considers Katz too low in status to challenge to a duel, so the aristocrat hires some toughs to work the artist over. The beating leaves

Katz partially paralyzed, which does little to affect his output and curiously seems to make him more attractive to some women. In 1938 Fritz Lang directs a film about Katz starring Peter Lorre—who has a certain resemblance to Katz—and a little-known Austrian actress whose stage name is simply Sarah. It receives rave reviews, but its full frontal nudity is controversial. The film is banned in Boston and some other American cities, drawing even larger crowds to those theaters where it plays.

In the historical world most American orchestras were under the batons of European conductors until the 1960s. Pierre Monteaux (France) conducted in Boston, Arturo Toscanini (Parma) and Bruno Walter (Berlin) in New York, Eugene Ormandy (Budapest) in Philadelphia, Erich Leinsdorff (Vienna) and George Szell (Budapest) in Cleveland, Antal Doráti (Budapest) in Dallas and Detroit, Fritz Reiner (Budapest) in Cincinnati and Chicago, and Otto Klemperer (Breslau) in Los Angeles (until 1939). Leonard Bernstein (1918–1990) was the most famous American-born conductor and about the only one to lead a major symphony orchestra before the 1960s. Prominent Europeans—including the violinists Jascha Heifetz (Lithuania) and Nathan Milstein (Russia), cellists Gregor Piatigorsky (Russia) and Janos Starker (Hungary), and pianists Arthur Rubinstein (Russian Poland) and Vladimir Horowitz (Russia)—also dominated the performing world. Had neither World War I nor the Russian Revolution occurred, most of these soloists would have remained in Europe, giving concerts all over the Continent, including my favorite venue, Bechstein Hall, on Wigmore Street in London. The eponymous German piano company built the hall and had its showroom next door; at the height of anti-German feeling during World War I it was renamed Wigmore Hall.

Rudolf Bing (Austria) ruled the Metropolitan Opera from 1952 to 1970 and worked with Arturo Toscanini and Bruno Walter as his principal conductors. He hired such American singers as Marian Anderson, Reri Grist, Robert Merrill, and Shirley Verret, and he fostered the careers of Roberta Peters, Leontyne Price, Grace Bumbry, Anna Moffo, Sherrill Milnes, and Jess Thomas. Bing nevertheless had a preference for Europeans, and during his tenure, the Met's headliners included Ezio Pinza, Maria Callas, Renata Tebaldi, Montserrat Caballé, Birgit Nilsson, Elisabeth Schwartzkopf, Carlo Bergonzi, Placido Domingo, Luciano Pavarotti, and Jon Vickers.

In my better world Bing grows up in Vienna and becomes a patient of Sigmund Freud's. This is not far-fetched as most of his patients came from Jewish professional families. One of Freud's most famous cases was that of "Little Hans," a young boy who was afraid of horses, which Freud, after analyzing his dreams and conversations, attributed to Hans's Oedipal complex. Little Hans turned out to be Herbert Graf, who later became a well-known American opera impresario. Gustav Mahler, appointed conductor of the Vienna Court Opera (Hofoper) in 1897, had to convert to Catholicism to secure this post. His protégé Bruno Walter followed suit. The Jewish Bing is also younger, and conversion is no longer necessary, although he is highly assimilated and marries a ballerina from a Catholic family. Bing pursues a long career as an impresario at the court opera and manages productions at the Salzburg and Glyndebourne festivals as well. Mahler and Walter also remain in Vienna, although they are frequent guest conductors in New York. Without Mahler, Walter, Bing, Toscanini, and a host of other European musical figures, America's classical music scene is much impoverished. Russia's, in contrast, is improved, as the composers Sergei Prokofiev and Igor Stravinsky and the choreographer Sergei Diaghilev stay in Russia, although they are frequent visitors to Paris. In a noncommunist Russia, Stalin does not terrorize Dmitri Shostakovich, compelling the composer to write music acceptable to the dictator. Shostakovich's compositions are accordingly more abstract. He writes fewer symphonies and more string quartets. Many connoisseurs rank the latter as equal to those of Haydn, Mozart, Beethoven, and Schubert.

The United States is impoverished in a second sense. Five of the American singers brought along by Bing are African American. In this less tolerant alternative world, Bing tries and largely fails to launch their national careers. Most are consigned to singing in lesser venues or churches, and they bring their classical training to gospel. Prejudice also affects the development of popular music. In the historical world, rock 'n' roll developed from African American music, played on white radio stations after being altered by white bands like Bill Haley and the Comets to appeal to white audiences. Some version of this transpires, but the white record market and radio stations do not open up to black performers. Soul music and Motown, or its equivalent, appeal to and are produced for largely black audiences.

Literature in the alternative world has many important differences in emphasis, as more European writers stay in place, and others, who died in the war or flu pandemic, survive and lead long and productive lives. American writers continue to follow Henry James and T. S. Eliot to London. As European culture is upbeat, the pessimism, nostalgia, and elitism of Eliot and Ezra Pound do not have wide appeal, although both poets are admired for their technical skills. Pound is as unstable as he was in the historical world, but in the absence of a world war, he does not become disillusioned with England, flirt with Fascism, and move to Italy. He accordingly avoids being arrested for treason in 1945 after denouncing the United States on Rome Radio, is not locked up for twenty-five days in a steel cage, and does not have a nervous breakdown. He nevertheless is a racist and condemns the civil rights movement as a Jewish plot.

In the absence of two world wars, literary interchange is more international, more concerned with regional and universal questions. Nationalism has increasingly become the banner under which demagogues attempt to mobilize political support among those opposed to the secular values of modernity or those excluded from its economic benefits. Western European writers, most of whom are liberal, turn against nationalism and parody its pretensions. Others embrace local idioms and customs to combat the impersonal nature of a mass, increasingly globalized, society. Following Johann Gottfried von Herder, most value all cultures, not just their own, and use their characters and local settings to probe universal traits and problems. As English is not the lingua franca, translation is more commonplace than in our world, making it easier for those who write in languages other than English, Spanish, French, and German to reach worldwide audiences.

However, important national differences in tradition and style remain. They are most evident in Russia, whose literary trajectory differs the most from that in our historical world. Absent World War I, the Soviet Union, Stalin's purges, and World War II, more writers survive, and those who do are less likely to emigrate. They escape the dead hand of Socialist realism and, along with composers and artists, are allowed to explore diverse modern pathways. In short they are not cut off from the mainstream of European cultural development and make substantial contributions to it. The circle of intellectuals surrounding Mikhail Bakhtin, the great theorist of internal dialogue, produce highly original readings of great poems and novels that resonate with Western writers, who are already deeply engaged with introspection.

Russian intellectuals develop a mystical and anti-Western orientation. Nineteenth-century Russian nationalism stressed moral over material forces and contrasted the holy mission of the Russian people to Western rationalism and materialism. Russian nationalism emphasized the communal life of the Rus in contrast to the individualism of the West. Aleksei S. Khomiakov, Konstantin S. Aksakov, and Fyodor Dostoevsky were among those who propagated the belief that Russia had inherited the Christian ideal of universal spiritual unification from Byzantium, whereas the decadent West, formed in the crucible of Roman Catholicism, preserved the old Roman imperial tradition. As Russia is the least advanced economically of the major powers and the most culturally insecure, this tradition is maintained and continues to find expression.

In the historical world the tradition of Russian nationalism was kept alive in the Soviet-and post-Soviet-era writings of Alexander Solzhenitsyn. In the better world he is a minor writer, respected for his literary skills but relatively isolated because of his political views. Mikhail Bulgakov and Andrei Platonov become Russia's best-known writers. Bulgakov never serves in the First World War and therefore is not badly wounded and does not become addicted to drugs or contract typhus. He still trains as a doctor and writes plays and novels that combine satire and science fiction, although war is not their principal subject. His more interesting plays, about Molière and Pushkin, are widely performed, not banned, as they were by Stalin. His best-known historical work—*The Master and Margarita*—is a biting satire of the Soviet system written in 1928 but not published until 1966. He does, however, produce a thinly veiled fictional critique of the strongman regime that emerges in Russia in the 1920s and of unintended and sometimes comic, sometimes tragic, consequences of the behavior of self-serving, ambitious, and generally unscrupulous people who do its bidding. It is quickly translated into multiple languages and is the basis of a prize-winning and popular film produced by Fritz Lang. Thanks to the novel and film, the neologism *kleptocrat* enters most Western languages.

At the other end of the spectrum are writers who free themselves entirely of the heavy hand of Russian history and culture. They turn to modernist literature and later help develop postmodernism. Their most original contribution may be in science fiction, a genre that emerged in Britain and France in the late nineteenth century but would find its greatest expression in twentieth-century Russia and America. Literary critics speculate that science fiction had great appeal in both countries for different reasons. In the United States, the most technologically advanced country, writers naturally embraced the new and the future. In Russia, in contrast, science fiction was a way to leave the past and backwardness behind.

Russia's greatest science fiction writer is Isaak Yudovitš Ozimov (known in our world as Isaac Asimov). He was born in 1919 or 1920 in a small Russian town near the border of today's Belarus. In our better world his parents do not emigrate to the United States when he is three years old but instead stay in Russia. He grows up speaking Yiddish and Russian instead of Yiddish and English. His parents are Orthodox Jews, but his father is remarkably tolerant of his son's secular orientation. From an early age Isaak develops an interest in science and begins reading translated science fiction stories. This provides a strong incentive for him to learn English, the language in which so many of these stories are written. He excels in school and wins a scholarship to an institute of electrical engineering in Kiev. After his studies, he works for the government authority charged with constructing a national power grid and bringing electricity to rural regions of the country. He publishes his first science fiction story while a student, and his output increases significantly after graduation.

Ozimov wrangles a posting for himself in Odessa, the home of Russian science fiction writing and publishing. Within a few years he has earned enough from his stories and novels—mostly from foreign rights—to quit his day job and devote himself full time to reading and writing. He writes books on a wide range of topics, fiction and nonfiction. His histories of science and technology and biographies of Pushkin and Tolstoy are best sellers, as are his science fiction works. He also produces Russian translations of Conan Doyle's Sherlock Holmes adventures. Among science fiction fans, he is best known for his series of novels about robots and an empire set in the distant future. The robot novels are inspired by the Czech author Cyril Karel Čapek's *R.U.R.*, published in 1921. Čapek's human-like robots free humans from work but rebel against their servitude and kill all the people they can except for Alquist, a clerk and the only human who still works with his hands. In his novels, Ozimov's robots are programmed to follow laws that make them incapable of rebelling against their masters, but humans, protective of what they think of as their unique status, are unwilling to give robots equal rights even in their Socialist society. Change occurs when robots and humans begin to breed, initially bringing revulsion and violence against those responsible for such miscegenation but ultimately compelling recognition and acceptance. The novels are read as not-so-veiled attacks on anti-Semitism in Europe and racial injustice in the United States.

The four empire novels are about the decline and rebirth of a galactic empire but also the survival of a much maligned but creative ethnic group, told through successive life stories of family members. The novels represent the tensions between, but also the coming together of, the author's dual identifications as Jewish and Russian. Farther west, especially in the United States, these identifications are more compatible, even reconcilable. Anti-Semitism is rife in Russia, although nothing like it was in the historical world at the time of the Russian Revolution. Like their czarist predecessors, central authorities often ignore violence against Jews or even encourage it. Many of Ozimov's contemporaries embrace socialism or Zionism in the hope of resolving their dilemma psychologically and politically. Ozimov opts for assimilation, hoping in the long run that it will prove the most viable strategy. His empire novels show how this can be made to work in a political system, and society, that is in many ways like Russia.

Slavophil nationalists considered Russia the third Rome—after Rome and Byzantium—and the true inheritors of Caesar's mantle. Ozimov's novels depict the collapse of a civilization loosely modeled on Byzantium; the collapse is followed by a dark age and the rise of competing political units, one of which represents the West in its emphasis on rationality and science. The other is more communal, religious, and mystical, intended as a futuristic version of Russia. The two societies ultimately blend, much to the advantage of both, a process facilitated by the inside-outside status of the ethnic minority in both societies. The ethnic group itself is deeply divided between those with secular scientific orientations and those with religious mystical ones, just like Russian Jews of Ozimov's era. Some readers purport to find hints of Yiddish sentence structure in the dialog among key characters. The more universal message of the novels is the extent to which people in the distant future, with undreamed-of technologies at their disposal, confront the same kinds of problems that human beings always have.

Ozimov was poorly coordinated; he never learned to ride a bicycle. He was afraid of heights and preferred to be confined. This may account for his pronounced fear of flying. He worked in a cramped office, which he loved, and had a decided preference for small, tucked-away hotel rooms when on the road. As a well-known author and excellent lecturer in German and English, he received invitations from all over the world but refused those that were not within convenient reach of trains. He once visited the United States, coming over on the *Queen Elizabeth,* given a free first-class cabin in return for a series of lectures. His first marriage ended in divorce, and he never remarried. As a culture figure with a gregarious personality, he found it easy to meet women and achieved a reputation as a roué. He died of a heart attack at the age of seventy-seven.

SCIENCE AND SOCIAL SCIENCE

In the historical world Germany had ceased to be the center of physics by 1945. So had Copenhagen, as most of its physicists had fled the Nazi occupation. The Cavendish Laboratory at Cambridge made the wise decision to concentrate less on physics and more on biology because the war-ravaged and impoverished British economy could not afford the kind of atom smashers that might have kept physicists competitive with the Americans in the field of particle physics. Most important work in almost all fields of physics would now be done in the United States and the Soviet Union. As of 2011 Americans had won 47 percent of all the Nobel Prizes in the sciences, medicine, and economics. From 1952 on, hardly a year went by when an American did not win the physics prize, for a total of seventy-eight awards. In physiology and medicine US dominance is even more striking, with a total of eighty-nine awards since 1946. Germany also lost dominance in mathematics. Before Hitler the dominant math journal in the world was the *Zentralblatt für Mathematik und ihre Grenzgebiete;* today the leading journals are all in English. Of the top eight contemporary math institutes in the world, three are located in the United States, none in Germany.

In April 1962 President John F. Kennedy invited to dinner at the White House forty-six American Nobelists and some foreign prize holders who were visiting or working in the United States. Never at a loss for words, the president quipped, "I think this is the most extraordinary collection of talent, of human knowledge, that has ever been gathered together at the White House, with the possible exception of when Thomas Jefferson dined alone."

In our better world many American physicists do graduate work or accept postdocs and professorships in Cambridge, Heidelberg, Berlin, or Copenhagen. European scientists for the most part remain on their continent, although many visit the United States, and a few emigrate, attracted by high pay and special research opportunities. This difference is effectively illustrated by the actual and counterfactual careers of five extraordinary Jewish graduates of the Budapest-Fasori Evangélikus Gimnázium: Edward Teller, John Harsanyi, John von Neumann, Leo Szilard, and Eugene Wigner. They studied with Lászlo Rátz, by all accounts an inspiring teacher of mathematics. The gymnasium, founded in 1823 by the Lutheran Church, attracted many Jewish students, among them Theodor Herzl, Georg Lukács, and Antal Doráti.

In the real world John von Neumann, born in 1903, did pioneering work in mathematics, game theory, economics, programming, statistics, numerical analysis, ergodic theory, set theory, and functional analysis. Hans Bethe, who won the Nobel for discovering the helium cycle that powers fusion in stars, offered Neumann as "evidence that a higher species of human was possible." Before emigrating to the United States and Princeton, Neumann worked in Göttingen and Berlin. He was a highly cultured man, spoke Greek and Latin, among other languages, was an authority on Byzantine history, and could recite much of Goethe's *Faust* from memory.

In our alternative world von Neumann remains in Germany and works closely with the circle of great physicists and mathematicians at Heidelberg, Göttingen, and Berlin. He is a clotheshorse and dresses formally, even on hikes in the woods. He is a great socializer, a party animal, and a lover of food. According to his wife, he can count anything but calories. He loves off-color stories and Yiddish jokes, both of which he exchanges with his closest buddy, the Polish mathematician Stanislaw Ulam, who works in Göttingen. Von Neumann is a gentle man but a terror on the roads and has numerous accidents. In one crash Albert Einstein and Niels Bohr were his passengers and were miraculously uninjured. The authorities finally revoke his license. In the real world von Neumann died at fifty-seven from bone cancer, which may have been the result of his attendance at the 1946 Bikini Atoll atomic tests. In the alternative world he lives into his seventies and makes additional contributions to mathematics, physics, and information technology.

Leo Szilard, born in 1898, conceived of the idea of the nuclear chain reaction while crossing a London street, and he went on to develop the first nuclear reactor with Enrico Fermi. He independently invented the electron microscope and the cyclotron and with Einstein coauthored the famous 1939 letter that convinced FDR to authorize the Manhattan Project and production of the world's first atomic bombs. Szilard had a confidence that proved essential to the construction of the first atomic pile, or reactor, as it is now called, at the University of Chicago. His calculations showed that graphite would be the ideal moderator of neutrons. When the graphite rods did not work out as planned, he reasoned this could only be because the government, despite the insistence of the National Bureau of Standards, had not supplied sufficiently pure graphite. With purer graphite the pile went critical. In real life Szilard never won the Nobel Prize, but other physicists considered his one of the most fertile minds in the profession.

Szilard spent hours every day in the bath thinking but always had time—as I know from my University of Chicago experience—to shoot the breeze with his students. After the war he was a cofounder of the antiwar *Bulletin of the Atomic Scientists* and a tireless campaigner against nuclear weapons. Toward the end of his life, when he was battling bladder cancer, he published a book of short stories. The opening tale is about a breakthrough that allows scientists to communicate with dolphins, which turn out to be more intelligent than humans. They help scientists solve a series of difficult problems, leading to inventions that enormously benefit humankind. These breakthroughs really are the collaborative efforts of Western and Soviet bloc scientists but are attributed to dolphins, who insist that they will continue to work with humanity only if Washington and Moscow end their Cold War.

Wigner Jenő Pál, as Eugene Wigner was known in Budapest, was born in 1902. He was corecipient of the Nobel physics prize in 1963 for his theoretical contributions to particle physics, especially the discovery and application of fundamental symmetry principles. He also did significant work in mathematics. In real life he left Germany for Princeton, where he had a long career. Late in life he developed an interest in Hindu philosophy and was drawn to its conception of the universe as an all-pervasive consciousness. He insisted that the laws of quantum mechanics could not be formulated in a consistent way without reference to consciousness.

Teller Ede (Edward Teller), born in 1908, is the youngest of the Hungarian physics foursome. He did not speak a word until he was three years old, prompting his grandfather to try to help his daughter adjust to having produced an imbecile. Teller later claimed he remained silent because his father spoke Hungarian but poor German and his mother the reverse. He concluded that neither knew what they were talking about and took refuge in numbers. He would perform all kinds of mental calculations. He remembered working out how many seconds there are in a year.

Eager to escape Hungary's authoritarian regime and restrictions against Jews, Teller left for Germany in 1926. In Munich he lost his right foot when he was run over by a tram. He studied physics with Werner Heisenberg in Leipzig and, through the good offices of Teller's Czech friend George Placek, found a summer job in Rome with Enrico Fermi. This experience convinced Teller to devote his career to nuclear physics. He subsequently spent time in Cambridge and in Copenhagen with Niels Bohr. In 1934 he married the sister of a long-time friend. He emigrated to the United States in 1936 and worked on the Manhattan Project at Los Alamos. Almost from the beginning Teller pushed for the development of a thermonuclear, as opposed to an atomic, device and became known as the father of the hydrogen bomb. He made numerous contributions to nuclear physics and spectroscopy.

In contrast to most of the physics community, Teller was right wing politically. At the onset of the Cold War he was keen to develop the hydrogen bomb and became a willing adviser to Republican presidents. He testified against J. Robert Oppenheimer, falsely accused of being a Communist, or at least a security risk, by J. Edgar Hoover's FBI. Teller became something of a pariah to most of the physics community. He had a notorious temper and was a difficult individual, but he loved to entertain friends with his impressive renditions of Beethoven piano sonatas. He is generally considered to have been the model for Dr.

Strangelove, the mad scientific genius of the eponymous 1964 movie that starred Peter Sellers.

Harsányi János Károly was an economist best known for his contributions to game theory and its application to economics. A utilitarian, he attempted to apply game theory to political and moral philosophy. He was corecipient of the Nobel in economics in 1994.

In our better world none of these scientists becomes Americans. They stay in Europe, where they study and work with the likes of Max Planck (b. 1858), Lise Meitner (b. 1878), Albert Einstein (b. 1879), Otto Hahn (b. 1879), Abram Ioffe (b. 1880), Niels Bohr (b. 1885), Erwin Schrödinger (b. 1886), A. A. Fridman (b. 1888), Wolfgang Pauli (b. 1900), Werner Heisenberg (b. 1901), Enrico Fermi (b. 1901), Paul Dirac (b. 1902), Pyotr Kapitsa (b. 1904), Hans Bethe (b. 1906), and Lev Landau (b. 1908).

With no war they avoid disruption and personal tragedies. The physicist Max Planck profits more than most. His first wife died in 1909, his two daughters died while giving birth in 1917 and 1919, one son was killed in World War I in 1916, and the other was executed in 1944 for plotting against Hitler. At the very least his sons would have survived, and perhaps his daughters, had they given birth in better health in peacetime conditions. Planck won the Nobel Prize in 1918, and his quantum theory, along with Einstein's theory of relativity, gave birth to modern physics. Planck's work life also would have been different if war had never broken out. He spent most of his career at the University of Berlin and was president of the Kaiser Wilhelm Society for the Promotion of Science until 1937, when he clashed with the Nazis. Planck stayed in Germany during World War II, but Allied bombing destroyed his house, and he had to be rescued by American forces at the end of the war.

To our list of famous physicists we must add promising young men who died in World War I. The English physicist Henry Moseley was killed at Gallipoli in 1915. He had already done work worthy of a Nobel in his empirical justifications of physical and chemical laws and by delineating what is known as Moseley's law in the X-ray spectra. The German Karl Schwarzschild died of disease on the Russian front in 1916. The year before, he had come up with the first known solution to Einstein's field equations for general relativity for the limited case of a single spherical nonrotating mass. The Viennese physicist Friedrich Hasenöhrl died in a grenade attack while fighting Italians in the Tyrol. He was Schrödinger's professor and made an important contribution to the development of relativity. Then, of course, we must ponder the contributions never made by younger men who died in uniform before they had a chance to finish university or graduate training.

These physicists and their students circulate around Europe, spending time as students, postdocs, and faculty in Cambridge, Amsterdam, Copenhagen, Rome, Zurich, Munich, Heidelberg, Göttingen, Berlin, and Leipzig. They are multilingual, and most develop a commitment to science that transcends national identity. As a group they are committed to peace and the kind of liberal order that fosters freedom in thinking and expression and personal geographic mobility. Most are aloof from politics but become increasingly aware of the military implications of their research. In the 1930s, as in the historical world, Leo Szilard imagines the nuclear reactor and with it the potential to produce enriched plutonium that could be used to create a bomb of unimagined destruction. In our better world, in advance of the ninth Solvay Conference in 1951, he quietly consults with Bohr, Einstein, Planck, Meitner, and Ioffe, all of whom quickly agree that such a weapon should never be developed. They sound out younger colleagues and discuss the matter behind closed doors for two days. They are unanimous that fission should be exploited for peaceful scientific purposes only. Many physicists, however, object to doing anything in secret, as it violates the ethical nature of their enterprise.

Bohr and Einstein offer a compromise that all accept after further debate. Everyone present will sign a public pledge never to work on weapons development of any kind and to circulate the petition among their colleagues to collect as many signatures as possible. Einstein, Bohr, and Szilard will host a press conference at which they will explain this decision and the scientific reasons for thinking that a chain reaction of neutrino release could unleash extraordinary energy. They will seek funding from governments and foundations to explore this line of research with the goal of exploiting fission for science and whatever practical benefits might accrue. The research funds will be awarded by a new foundation, and all research must be conducted openly and be monitored by an organization set up for the purpose. The Belgian government, neutral and a cohost of the conference, sounds out other governments, and a consortium comprised of Britain, Belgium, Holland, Denmark, Italy, Germany, and Austria-Hungary is soon formed. Sometime later Russia and the United States join, but Japan does not. The first atomic pile is built in Denmark, in honor of Niels Bohr, and comes online in 1941.

The social sciences mirror their physics counterpart in important ways. The rise of Fascism brought a flood of social scientists across the Atlantic to enrich US universities and their intellectual life. In my field of international relations the United States had only two prominent theorists between the world wars: Quincy Wright and Harold Lasswell, both at the University of Chicago for most of their careers. Lasswell was born and raised on an Illinois farm. He pioneered the study of public opinion and the field of political psychology, and he was much influenced by Sigmund Freud. The leading postwar theorists were Hans Morgenthau, John Herz, and Karl Deutsch, the first two refugees from Germany and the third from Prague (Austria-Hungary, later Czechoslovakia). When I was a student at the University of Chicago in the late 1950s and early 1960s, a significant percentage of my professors were of central European origin. With only some exaggeration I tell people that until I did graduate study, I thought *Plato* was pronounced "Plaato" and *Thucydides* "Tukidides," although at Yale I studied with Karl Deutsch, who also had a pronounced accent.

In our better world almost all these scholars stay in Europe. Universities and research centers in central Europe dominate the world of social science. Americans continue to do much of their graduate education in Europe, but many return to the United States and train the next generation of students. Gradually American social science develops into something substantial in its own right, much the way its Continental counterpart took two generations to regenerate after World War II. This secondary status has a bright side, which is that American graduate students, in addition to learning statistics, must master foreign languages. To study with leading figures on the Continent, they must learn German, just the way contemporary German, Dutch, and Scandinavian students today must be fluent English speakers. Learning other languages and spending years abroad familiarize American students with other cultures, and not infrequently they find local partners. In contrast to today's mathematically sophisticated but generally parochial social scientists, US scholars in this better world are more cosmopolitan and cultured, and it shows in their theories, choice of methods, and epistemological commitments.

RELIGION

Western Europe is largely secular in the historical world. Public opinion polls show that less than one-quarter of its population believes in a deity. The percentage is higher in eastern Europe, most notably in Poland and Ukraine, and slightly higher in Britain because of its large numbers of Muslim immigrants from South Asia. In Japan and the Pacific Rim belief is significantly less pronounced. The outlier is the United States, where more than 90 percent of the adult population routinely affirms its belief in god. Something like 70 percent also believe in heaven, but only 45 percent believe in hell. Within the United States belief in god is much more pervasive in rural than in urban areas, and in the South and Midwest. It is highest in the so-called Bible Belt, which runs in a crescent from West Virginia through Oklahoma. More blacks than whites believe in god, but this distinction disappears when we control for place of residence and level of education.

These percentages are only marginally lower in our better world, but they are enough to account for some significant differences. In Spain, which has not seen civil war but has seen a gradual liberalization, the civic culture is much different than in our world. No dramatic swing from a church-dominated society to a secular one in which gay marriage is legal has occurred. In Italy church-state relations were shaped by the Concordat, which Mussolini reached with the Vatican in 1929. Any dictator would have reached some kind of agreement along these lines, so the heavy hand of conservative popes continues to influence Italian educational and social policy. North of the Alps the principal exception to secularization is Bavaria, which is more Catholic in the better world. In the absence of a divided Germany, Munich does not need to become a substitute for the cultural and scientific centers, like Jena and Leipzig, which ended up in the German Democratic Republic. Bavaria and Munich are wealthy but have a smaller percentage of residents from elsewhere in Germany and the former Reich than they do in our world. In France and northern Europe churches of all denominations have lost membership and influence, although a few still receive state funding. Religion has become a shell, and churches are more likely to be visited by tourists than worshippers. Secular humanism is the dominant belief system, which helps to mute tensions in countries like Germany and Hungary, where religious divides were once pronounced and politicized.

Religion is most alive among Catholics and Muslim immigrants. Reformist and reactionary popes seem to alternate, almost as if by agreement, and each has different and partisan followings. Sermons against birth control, premarital sex, and homosexuality alienate liberal Catholics, and the church, as in the historical world, increasingly turns to Africa and Asia for new believers, priests, and nuns. This process begins several decades earlier and is much more pronounced by the end of the twentieth century. European and North American Catholics represent a much smaller and increasingly powerless segment of the church.

The first African pope, Isaac Obufame, is elected in 1980. He is a Nigerian orphan who was looked after and schooled by missionaries and then sent abroad for university and religious training. He is undeniably brilliant, having finished at the top of his class in every educational institution he attended. He is also humble and beloved by the Africans and others to whom he has ministered in the course of his career. Rumors circulate in Nigeria that he has been responsible for miracle cures, which he consistently denies. To discourage local veneration of him while still a young priest, he is given an administrative position in Rome and quickly becomes indispensable. In the next two decades he makes important theological contributions, becomes a speechwriter for two popes, and as a cardinal is a close adviser to the pope and serves as the church's principal spokesman for African affairs. At age sixty-two he becomes the youngest pope elected in modern times. He accelerates missionary activities in Africa and Asia and frequently reminds Catholics that Africans were prominent among early Christians—the most prominent example is St. Augustine of Hippo—and that Africa and Asia are where their religion will find its future. In his first decade in office he appoints a large number of non-European cardinals to reflect this shift in attention and membership.

In the United States evangelical Protestantism is increasingly dominant in the hinterland and among poor urban dwellers. White and black evangelicals are committed to conservative social values but differ on economic issues and civil rights. In response to evangelical pressures many states ban the teaching of evolution or make schools give equal billing to so-called creationism. Various evangelical sects, most notably Dispensationalism, periodically predict the rapture to heaven of true Christians, the second coming of Jesus, and even the end of the earth. Repeated failures of these predictions do little to diminish the appeal of millennialism. Believers also seem impervious to the numerous sexual and financial scandals that engulf leading evangelical ministers.

The most successful of these pastors—for a time at least—is a Californian by the name of Richard Milhous Nixon. Brought up as a conservative Quaker in a family that opposed drinking, card playing, dancing, and swearing, he received a scholarship to Harvard. In the real world he had to turn it down and attend the local Whittier College because his brother Harold contracted tuberculosis, and the family incurred great medical expenses. In our better world Harold avoids TB, which he had contracted from close association with a veteran who picked it up in France, and Richard goes to Harvard. He is bright and hardworking but feels uncomfortable in this liberal eastern establishment institution. Other students shun him as a square and a hick, and he finds fellowship in a small evangelical student association. He meets his future wife at a prayer meeting and, at her urging and with her family's financial support, commits himself to a career as a Methodist minister. Once ordained, he serves a couple of small parishes in southern California but is restless and deeply ambitious. He is attracted to radio evangelism as a means of reaching more people and winning a larger following, but he is not a spellbinding speaker and cannot really bring himself to talk with conviction about fire and brimstone.

Nixon turns briefly to a political career and wins election to Congress, where he combines social conservatism with a mildly progressive economic outlook. He serves two undistinguished terms and is defeated by an unprincipled Democratic demagogue who in the last days of the election campaign barrages residents with leaflets accusing Nixon of sexual relationships with unnamed teenage girls in his church. Nixon is outraged and honestly denies any wrongdoing, but the damage has been done. He makes an emotional and angry concession speech that effectively ends his political career. For six months he is deeply depressed but emerges convinced he has been chosen by god to carry forward his message of forgiveness and Christian love. He finds backers to invest in a large, modern church building, promising them a good return on their investment. He buys time on a local radio station after spending months honing his message and improving his delivery style. He is remarkably successful, which he takes as proof of god's support, and he has little difficulty convincing various companies to back his broadcasts with their advertising dollars.

Nixon's message is largely autobiographical: humble beginnings, love of god, and rejection of secularism bring material success. Sometimes he preaches while sitting at the piano and augments his sermons with religious tunes he composes. His approach is tremendously appealing to upwardly mobile and educated evangelicals. His listening audience grows exponentially, as does his wealth and that of his backers, when he offers to say special prayers for listeners who make contributions to his Church of Prosperity. Nixon franchises his church and takes a cut of all proceeds. He is intellectually sophisticated, and although he never preaches doctrine, he is able to provide listeners with arguments to use against faithless liberals. He avoids all sexual scandals, unlike so many other evangelists, and his wife, Susan, becomes a role model for other college-educated evangelical women. She continues to dress simply—in her famous cloth coat—despite the couple's wealth.

Nixon is not content with his empire and is fiercely jealous of another evangelist, the scion of an upper-class Republican family in New York who has also built a phenomenally successful radio ministry. Reading between the lines of his rival's sermons, which Nixon carefully studies, he becomes convinced that the New Yorker is out to get him and is the source of rumors that circulate about Nixon and financial improprieties. Nixon has assistants break into the other evangelist's office, rifle his files, and leave a microphone in place to record his conversations. The assistants also pull off a number of dirty tricks intended to make the press and public believe that Nixon's rival is an alcoholic and closet transvestite. Reporters are tipped to the scheme by one of Nixon's henchmen, who feels guilty about his participation. An investigation by the *New York Times* exposes the truth. Nixon continually denies wrongdoing and attempts to blame his trouble on liberal journalists who hate him and Jesus. His lies and his unsuccessful efforts at a cover-up alienate more people than his initial misbehavior. He is forced to step down from the pulpit. Several of his supporters are convicted of felonies, and one, another minister, becomes a reforming politician after serving his prison time.

Muslims are religious but much less extreme in their social and political views than their historical counterparts. Colonialism has lasted longer, but some countries, notably India and Egypt, have made a gradual transition to self-rule. Nationalist movements and ethnic competition have produced considerable turmoil but nothing like the civil wars and ethnic cleansing associated with independence and postindependence regimes in the real world. Africans and Asians alike are accordingly healthier, better educated, and wealthier. Birthrates, while high, are lower throughout the second half of the twentieth century than they were historically.

Colonial administrations are better and worse than independent governments. They are disliked for reserving most important positions for Europeans and for paying them more for the same work. They also give preference to European economic interests, which often operate in colonies without the kinds of labor and environmental protections they must accommodate at home. They also pay less in taxes. On the positive side of the ledger, more and better schooling is available, especially in British, French, and German colonies, as are more scholarships to home country institutions of higher learning. Immigrants to the metropolises have better economic opportunities. In India, Egypt, and Malaya top administrative positions are increasingly occupied by locals who take pride in serving their peoples.

Dictatorships and kleptocracies are largely avoided. This makes South Asia and the Middle East radically different from anything we know. In South Asia Pakistan does not exist, as India has not been divided. The better world avoids partition and its associated bloodshed: four costly wars and a continuing struggle over Kashmir. India does not develop nuclear weapons, and Islamic militants are relatively powerless. In the Middle East Israel does not exist, so neither do Arab-Israeli disputes, and more progressive regimes rule Lebanon, Syria, Egypt, and North Africa. With better government and some chance of upward mobility, Islamic fundamentalism is restricted to regions like Arabia and Yemen. Lebanon becomes the wealthiest country in the Middle East and rivals western Europe in its per capita standard of living. Beirut is a major port and a crossroads for Western products coming east and Middle Eastern agricultural produce and raw materials, most notably oil, coming west. Major pipelines run to Beirut and Jaffa, in the Palestine protectorate. Religious Sunni and Shi'a Muslims; Armenian, Orthodox, and Coptic Christians; and Jews live in relative harmony. Their more secular counterparts tend to be nationalistic and continually at one another's throats.

With neither Hitler nor the Holocaust, the Jewish population of Europe prospers. During the twentieth century its center increasingly shifts west as Jews seek a better life and more educational opportunities. Within eastern Europe they make a similar move from shtetl to city. Yiddish survives as a spoken tongue with a thriving literature, although by the end of the century, it is no longer the primary language of most Jews. Eastern Europe's Jews were largely Orthodox in 1900, but secularization was well underway and accelerates as the century moves on. Traditional synagogues are nevertheless dotted throughout the region. Farther west, Jewish congregations are likely to be Reform (Liberal) and their members assimilated to their respective national cultures.

In the latter half of the nineteenth century, German Jews increasingly described themselves as "deutscher Staatsbürger jüdischen Glaubens" (Germans of the Jewish faith), and this model is adopted elsewhere. Judaism combines ethnicity and religion, and many of its holidays are as much historical as religious, so even secular Jews identify as Jewish, and most are proud of their cultural heritage. They give freely to charities organized to alleviate the plight of poorer Jews in the East and to ease their western migration, often to America.

The "Jewish Problem," as anti-Semites call it, has not gone away, and in some ways it has intensified. In eastern Europe nationalists were for the most part anti-Semitic and characterized Jews as a foreign element in their midst. However, during the twentieth century Jews gradually gain more acceptance. In the mid-nineteenth century Prince Metternich of Austria organized a coalition of great powers to pressure the Vatican to respect the liberties of Jews in its Italian territories. In the 1890s the great powers tried unsuccessfully to get the central government of the Ottoman Empire to refrain from violence against its Armenian population. In my better world the great powers—Germany, Austria-Hungary, France, Britain, and the United States—pressure eastern European governments to remove restrictive laws against Jews and treat them and other minorities more equitably. Western European peoples are nevertheless unhappy with sizable Jewish migration to their midst, and right-wing political parties make it a regular campaign issue. Responsive governments put informal barriers in place, and western European governments and Jewish charities alike encourage eastern European Jews to make new lives for themselves in the United States and Canada. This strategy creates tensions with Washington, as state governments have to cope with widespread anti-immigrant sentiment in the heartland. Despite these problems the Jewish population of

western Europe grows, and Jews make huge contributions to the economic, scientific, and cultural life of the entire Continent.

THRILLS AND CHILLS

Every world is entertained or threatened by unexpected developments
of all kinds. In the historical world the immediate post–World War I
decade witnessed the influenza pandemic, flappers, radio, Lindbergh's
solo flight across the Atlantic, and a few years later the kidnapping
and murder of his baby son. In 1936 Edward VII abdicated the British
throne. Also during the 1930s sports fans in Europe and America were
riveted by great contests in baseball, cricket, boxing, bicycle racing, and
the 1936 Berlin Olympics with its notable track-and-field events. The
highlight of the Olympics was the phenomenal running and jumping
of the black American athlete Jesse Owens, who won four gold medals.
Host Adolf Hitler failed to acknowledge Owens's victories and refused
to shake his hand. The 1940s were dominated by the world war, which
actually started in 1937 with the Japanese invasion of China. Many less
deadly events engaged postwar publics. They included the integration
of baseball, Elizabeth II's inauguration, Edmund Hillary and Tenzing
Norgay's successful assault on Everest in 1952, the Brooklyn Dodgers'
first World Series victory in 1955, and Sputnik in 1957. In the world of
entertainment Elvis Presley, Brigitte Bardot, Marilyn Monroe, Sophia
Loren, and Alec Guinness became headliners. Terms like hepcat, bebop,
beatnik, H-bomb, Salk vaccine, and pizza entered the American and
British lexicons or came into wider usage.

     In the space I have available, I cannot offer even a bare bones ac-
count of similar developments in my alternative world. It is equally rich
in human accomplishments, grand events, and pageantry, as well as

gripping adventures on and off the world's playing fields, golf courses, tennis courts, and tracks. More interesting than recounting the names and feats of otherwise unknown adventurers, entertainers, and athletes might be some observations about the ways in which adventure, entertainment, and sport differ in this better world. This requires great restraint because I must refrain from having the Dodgers and Giants stay in New York, the Red Sox win a World Series in 1946, 1967, 1976, 1986—or in all four—and Arsenal triumph consistently in key matches against the Hotspurs and Manchester United. "Man U" would also avoid the 1958 Munich air disaster that claimed twenty-three lives, including eight of its players.

I referred earlier to the film industry and how Hollywood fails to gain hegemony in my better world. Many of Hollywood's key figures stay in Europe, as they do not have to flee Fascists or Nazis. With no Great Depression the public has less need for escapist entertainment, and Hollywood can attempt to address more serious themes. Social conservatism is nevertheless stronger than in the historical world, and well until the 1960s the American movies are hobbled by production codes and racial constraints that liberals and Europeans find laughable or offensive. The British film industry prospers as it helps to fill a vacuum. Ealing Studios, famous in the 1950s for films like *Kind Hearts and Coronets, The Lavender Hill Mob,* and *The Ladykillers,* receives an infusion of American capital and comes to rival Warner Brothers, MGM, and 20th Century Fox.

As in the real world US customs officials routinely confiscate novels deemed pornographic—especially ones they want to take home and read—like D. H. Lawrence's *Lady Chatterley's Lover* but also European films that suggest sex between unmarried couples, imply the use of condoms, or show women's nipples, let alone full frontal nudity. American

Puritanism remains even more entrenched than in the historical world. A large black market in books and movies develops in the United States, facilitated by the outright refusal of some cities like New York to prosecute bookstores or theaters that sell or show banned products. Efforts by conservative national politicians to compel local authorities to close down this trade play well in the heartland but fail in practice as nonenforcement makes mayors and police chiefs more popular with their constituencies. College fraternities get their own copies of outlawed books and films, which make them an even bigger draw on campus. In libertarian New Hampshire, where "Live Free or Die" is the state motto, fraternities at Dartmouth exploit their greater freedom to establish a profitable mail-order business in illicit films and books. In 1956 the FBI raids two fraternities and touches off a huge political and legal battle.

In the chills department the frequency of mine shaft collapses and hotel fires is about the same. More train derailments, shipwrecks, and airplane crashes occur because radar and information technology are delayed. The two biggest generic changes concern nuclear power and storms. In the real world nuclear power has been a blessing and a curse. Thirty countries operate nuclear power plants, but only France uses them as a primary source of energy. The nuclear power industry has been plagued by disasters—Three Mile Island, Chernobyl, and Fukushima—and as this book goes to press, Germany and Switzerland are phasing out their nuclear power plants, and other countries are cutting back. In our alternative world nuclear power plants are less dangerous because the international consortium inspired by Bohr, Einstein, and Ioffe manages nuclear energy. It insists on extremely high standards of construction and inspection. The more serious problem is disposal of nuclear waste, an issue difficult to resolve for technical and political reasons. Energy demands are high; alternative sources to coal, oil, and nuclear power are still expensive but becoming increasingly competitive because European governments and Japan have made big investments in their development.

Weather is another matter. Globalization hastened economic development and with it global warming. More carbon dioxide is in the atmosphere, even with more reliance on alternative sources of energy. One consequence of global warming is more extreme weather of all kinds, so hurricanes, tornadoes, typhoons, and droughts are more pronounced. The water level is also higher because the polar ice caps are melting more rapidly. This compels the evacuation of some low-lying areas in Europe and Asia, and in today's Bangladesh, where this is impossible, millions die in devastating storms and floods. Other than some self-serving American capitalists, almost nobody denies the evidence of global warming, and the developed economies individually and collectively take initiatives to slow down and, they hope, reverse the effects of global warming. These agreements are possible only because the US government, while unhappy about these agreements, is not in a position to oppose them. The dominions of India and China also go along with environmental regulation in return for major concessions. However, whether global warming can be halted, let alone reversed, is still an open question.

The world does not escape the 1918–20 influenza pandemic, but fewer people die in Europe because young men are not so concentrated in armies and they are not so susceptible in the absence of war and the Allied blockade that caused conditions of near-starvation in Germany and Austria. In 1942 another outbreak of influenza that kills about 150 million people worldwide. Poliomyelitis remains a big killer, and intensifying outbreaks almost every summer through the 1950s began to rival the flu in their mortality. In our better world antibiotics are developed a decade later, so science does not overcome many common infections until the early 1960s. HIV reaches the Western world earlier, once again because of the effects of globalization. Because heroin use in North America and Europe is limited, needle transmission is a serious problem only among people who receive blood transfusions, and once known this means of transmission could easily be stopped through the use of clean blood and disposable needles. There is more resistance to this project in the better world than in ours.

Homosexuality and sexual promiscuity in general are the principal vectors for spreading HIV, and the United States has a much higher rate of infection than it does in the historical world because of the longer survival of Victorian sexual values. Homosexuality is taboo and still illegal in many states, and heterosexual prostitution, although illegal everywhere, is widespread. No federal funds are earmarked for HIV research because of conservative opposition in Congress, and the world as a whole has more difficulty coping with this scourge. Americans are shocked to learn of the deaths of some prominent actors and politicians who kept their sexual preferences and practices secret during their lifetime. The death from AIDS—initially announced as pneumonia—of a California senator hailed as a potential presidential contender serves as a catalyst to bring about a more open discussion of sexuality.

As the new century dawns, talking heads and public intellectuals around the world offer their assessments of the meaning of the twentieth century. Almost all hail the last hundred years as an era of unalloyed progress, most notably because it all but did away with the horror of interstate war. Knowing nothing about our world, they believe they have made great strides in racial and religious tolerance, medicine, and air travel. They welcome the prospect of space exploration—in the absence of a cold war the first human has set foot on the moon only recently—and what is starting to be called the information revolution. The head of a major international data-processing firm nevertheless insists that consumers will never be interested in purchasing personal computers.

5

The Worst Plausible World

A WORLD THAT AVOIDED THE SLAUGHTER OF 1914–18 probably would have been a more secure, wealthier, and peaceful world. How much better is impossible to know as all crystal balls are murky. Absent World War I, the world could have developed in ways that were neither obvious at the time nor necessarily obvious in retrospect. So any honest assessment of World War I and its consequences cannot limit itself to somewhat rosy futures. It requires a counterpoint narrative that explores darker possibilities.

The two worlds I create in this chapter are among the nastiest that I can plausibly conjure. The second is a variant of the first, and both diverge early on from the better world of chapters 3 and 4. The turning point is the constitutional development of Germany in the 1920s. Its evolution toward democracy paved the way for our better world. This development was highly contingent; it built on existing conditions but required a number of fortuitous developments. In their absence Germany could have developed differently and with it the rest of Europe.

In 1914 Germany had Europe's most educated and cultured population, relative freedom of the press, a strong labor movement, an elected parliament, and a bureaucracy and legal system widely regarded as honest and efficient. It was nevertheless a monarchy in which the kaiser exercised almost absolute powers over military and foreign policy as the parliament could not limit either by any means short of withholding funds for the court or military. The army and navy were also independent of civilian control and, like the kaiser, adamantly opposed to democracy. The German middle class was Europe's largest and strongly committed to material advancement. In contrast to its British, French, and Dutch counterparts, the German middle class was surprisingly feudal in its respect for hierarchy, authority, and everything military.

All these features were evident in World War I. The kaiser, Chancellor Bethmann-Hollweg, and Chief of Staff Helmuth von Moltke made the decision that led to war with Russia and France behind closed doors. They presented the parliament with a fait accompli, and it meekly went along; only four Socialists voted against the Burgfrieden that authorized war credits and imposed a moratorium on strikes for its duration. The war made inroads against class barriers as many non-aristocrats, of necessity, received commissions in line units. However, democracy as a whole suffered a serious setback. In November 1918 Germany was forced to sue for peace. The kaiser fled to Holland, and the Socialists proclaimed a republic on the steps of the Reichstag. Fearful of a Bolshevik-style uprising, the Socialists quickly made peace with the army, and the revolution was stillborn. The postwar Weimar Republic represented an uneasy compromise between pro- and anti-Republican forces and never succeeded in establishing legitimacy.

The war revealed the weakness of the socialist movement, not only in Germany but elsewhere in Europe, where workers rallied to

the national colors in preference to the red flag. Even when the Socialists took power in 1918, the Social Democratic Party (SPD) lacked the
courage to challenge the old order in any serious way. Trade unionists
were more interested in economic gains than political transformation.
The weakness, even spinelessness, of the German Left meant it unlikely
to contend in a showdown with the military.

It is by no means far-fetched to imagine a Germany and Europe
that avoid war and a German army that stages a coup against an aggressive parliament with the support, if not tacit backing, of the kaiser. The
court was dominated by officers with reactionary views. They would
have jumped on any opportunity to stage a coup, and a conflict like
the Zabern affair could have provided the context. The army would
have seen few, if any, defections, and the Prussian police would have
remained quiescent, as they did a little more than a decade later when
Hitler illegally asserted his authority over them.

A military coup would be followed by repression of the Left. The
army would have handled elections by vetting candidates in advance.
The military also would have asserted tighter control over the press,
universities, and the professions. The courts and bureaucracy would
have been compliant, as they were with Hitler. Some liberals would
have emigrated to France, Britain, and the United States, further weak-
ening the internal opposition to the military. The military would not
have tolerated expressions of nationalism by minority groups. Anti-
Semitism was rife and would have continued unabated. However, the
military had no interest in harassing Jews, did not do so during the war,
and would have regarded attacks against Jewish shops or synagogues as
expressions of civil disorder that had to be suppressed.

In 1914 German generals considered France their principal foe,
and its alliance with Russia confronted them with the prospect of a

two-front war. This prompted the Schlieffen Plan, which committed Germany to an all-out offensive against France, marching in through Belgium at the outbreak of war, in the hope of winning the war in the west before Russian forces could advance too deeply into Germany in the east. A more authoritarian Germany would have had strong reasons to seek better relations with Russia. Franz Ferdinand, who in our counterfactual world has survived his visit to Sarajevo and becomes emperor of Austria-Hungary in November 1916 following the death of Franz Josef, might have facilitated a rapprochement. He believed peace with Russia to be necessary to his empire's survival and had good personal relations with the Russian court. Russian authorities might have responded positively to any Austro-German overture to the extent that the Russians believed closer association with their conservative imperial neighbors was a useful way to strengthen the Russian regime and make it easier to suppress domestic opponents. An improvement in relations among the three eastern powers would not have solved Germany's military dilemma but would have made a war-threatening crisis much less likely.

Another distinct possibility is a revolution in Russia. In 1914 contemporary observers considered such an upheaval only a matter of time so long as the monarchy was unwilling to introduce democratic reforms. In our alternative world revolution breaks out and produces a parliamentary government, as it did initially in 1917. The ensuing Bolshevik coup attempt is crushed, and Lenin, Trotsky, and other Communists are killed or imprisoned. An imperfect democracy struggles to survive and ultimately gives way to rule by a strongman. Like Vladimir Putin, he uses his power over the government, business, and press to get his supporters elected to parliament and maintains the outward appearance of democracy.

In 1917 dissident nationalities, including Finns, Estonians, Lithuanians, Latvians, Poles, Ukrainians, and the peoples of the Caucasus, used the breakdown of order after the revolution to declare their independence. They would have done this again if the situation allowed. In the nineteenth century the three eastern empires had cooperated to repress nationalist uprisings, especially in Poland, and Berlin and Vienna probably would have aided Russia for fear that rebellion would spread to their own countries. Germany and Austria would have benefited from an intact but a weak Russia. It would have secured their eastern flanks strategically and allowed Germany to replace France as Russia's most important partner and gain access to grain, oil, and new markets.

A more authoritarian German regime would also have important implications for southern Europe. Italy was deeply divided by region, badly governed by short-lived coalitions, and dominated by self-serving politicians who catered to landlords and a few large business interests. Given its poor performance and the country's growing economic problems, democratic government was increasingly regarded as a failed experiment by much of the so-called Italian people. I say so called because most Italians had stronger regional than national identities. Political reform had little chance, and the labor movement became increasingly radicalized. The country was ripe for a coup even in the absence of war. It seems only a matter of time before Benito Mussolini or someone else built up an independent political-military base, marched on Rome—or took over a few northern cities—and coerced the country's weak king into making the strongman prime minister. Like Mussolini and Hitler, such a leader would quickly brush aside legal restraints to consolidate his dictatorship.

Italy was a great power in name only but harbored grand ambitions. It would have been unable to regain Italian-speaking lands under

Austrian rule, but one can readily imagine that Austria and Germany would encourage Italian imperial ambitions in the Mediterranean and Africa, as Hitler did in World War II. Such an imperial policy would have been popular in Italy and brought the country into conflict with France and Britain in the west and Albania and Greece in the east. Berlin would almost certainly have supported an Italian invasion of Abyssinia (Ethiopia), which would have raised tensions with Britain and France.

Spain and Portugal were the other western European states where democracy was fragile and where a more authoritarian Germany would have had an important impact. In the historical world both countries succumbed to dictatorships in the 1930s. Francisco Franco staged a military coup in Spain and became dictator after a bloody civil war. António de Oliveira Salazar became prime minister of Portugal legally and subsequently established a dictatorship. The two regimes were nationalist, corporatist, close to the Roman Catholic Church, and used the army and police to suppress opposition. They were even more natural allies of Germany, although both leaders would have kept their countries neutral in a war, as they did in World War II.

The other quasi-European great power to consider is the Ottoman Empire. In the historical world, the sultan was overthrown in 1908 in a coup sponsored by the Young Turks, a cabal of students and military cadets. In 1913 the Committee of Union and Progress, led by three pashas, seized power in response to the government's poor performance in the Second Balkan War. Known as the "Dictatorial Triumvirate," the pashas ruled until 1922. In my counterfactual world, in the absence of war this reformist and nationalist regime would have remained in power, fighting a rearguard campaign to maintain the former empire's lands in the Near East. Egypt, Libya, and Tunisia had already been lost, but the Arabs were weak and divided and incapable of liberating themselves without foreign support and Turkish military commitments elsewhere. Without World War I Britain would not have encouraged an Arab rebellion in Palestine or invaded it. Germany had good relations with the pashas and might have provided them the military aid they needed to maintain power and enforce Turkish authority throughout the Middle East.

In this world democracy is restricted to Switzerland, the Benelux countries, Scandinavia, France, Britain, and the overseas English-speaking world. Southern, central, and eastern Europe are governed by authoritarian nationalist, conservative regimes that maintain power by relying to varying degrees on censorship, their armies, and their secret police. Faced with a bloc of authoritarian regimes, France and Britain draw closer together, and the gulf between them and the other great powers widens.

The democracies are careful not to antagonize the German-dominated central European bloc, and Germany's generals recognize that they have little to gain from war. Suspicion and resentment are nevertheless rife. The Germans resent the refuge and succor Paris and London offer to socialist and other refugees from Continental authoritarianism. Berlin unsuccessfully attempts to pressure both governments to suppress the refugee press, which routinely publishes exposés and other unflattering articles and books about the German, Italian, Spanish, and Austrian governments and smuggles them across borders to the delight of its large readership. The United States does business with everyone, although the sympathies of its people and government are with the Western democracies. This is not a nice Europe, and most of its denizens live a cramped and uncomfortable life.

Darker scenarios readily spring to mind. They focus on deteriorating relations and intensifying conflict between the German bloc, which includes Austria and Italy, and the Anglo-French entente. Russia remains aloof although closer to Germany than to France. Japan, ruled by a military dictatorship, is a jackal waiting in the wings for an opportunity to feed on decaying imperial corpses in Asia.

London and Paris feel increasingly threatened by developments in Europe and Asia. They feel isolated and in decline relative to Germany. Berlin's construction of a blue water navy is not viewed kindly in London, where many politicians and strategists consider it a harbinger of a military challenge to come. Successive British governments accelerate their shipbuilding efforts and reach a secret understanding with the United States, as both London and Washington regard control of the sea as essential to their national security. They are equally troubled by the phenomenal growth of the Japanese navy and the political and military cooperation between it and Germany. Berlin sells increasingly sophisticated armaments to Tokyo, and the two countries exchange intelligence. By the late 1920s military observers from both countries are routinely embedded in each other's forces. By the 1940s Germany and Japan have a tacit alliance, cemented by frequent visits of high-ranking political and military officials and the cross training of junior officers.

Germans have a love-hate relationship with Britain. They envy London, its colonial and financial empires and the self-confidence of its leaders and political, business, and cultural elites. They want to equal its accomplishments and replace it as the leading European power. To a great extent this goal explains German investment in a navy, something costly and unnecessary for German security. Germans nonetheless regard battleships and colonies as the sine qua non of greatness, and what is at stake is not security but standing. Berlin also invests heavily in education and German-language instruction for foreigners for much the same reason. Had this competition remained largely symbolic,

Germany and the United Kingdom might have lived in peace. But the Germans use their newly developed power to bully others into recognizing their preeminence.

This was readily evident in three historical pre-1914 crises: the First and Second Moroccan Crises of 1904–5 and 1911–12 and the Bosnian annexation crisis of 1908–9. In the Moroccan crises Germany tried to coerce France into conceding colonies in return for recognizing a French protectorate in Morocco. Berlin's threats of war antagonized Paris and London and intensified German paranoia when the crisis brought the two long-time adversaries closer together. In the aftermath of the First Moroccan Crisis, the British and French armies drew up collaborative plans for a British expeditionary force to assist in the defense of France in the case of a German invasion.

In the worst world scenario another major European crisis erupts in 1918. It arises in conjunction with the Russian Revolution and attempts by non-Russian nationalities to establish their independence. Germany and Britain support opposing forces in this political-military contest between the Russian government and its periphery. France weighs in on the side of Britain, while Austria-Hungary backs Germany. Britain and France feel special sympathy for the Poles, and Paris has arranged to run arms to Polish rebels. The German navy stops one of the neutral ships France has been using to run arms and finds grenades, machine guns, and millions of rounds of bullets for the latter. The German government gives photographs of the boarding of the German press, which widely publicizes the French arms running. Denials in Paris only anger the Germans further, and they threaten to declare the Baltic a war zone and stop ships as they see fit.

Mussolini seeks to make a reputation as a statesman by mediating the dispute between Germany and France. Because no one wants war, the crisis is averted with no loss of face for either side. Another and more serious confrontation develops in regard to German penetration of Iran in search of secure oil and Germany's efforts, with Japan's help, to gain control of the Chinese railways and the economic benefits this would confer. The Iran crisis ends in a standoff, and the Chinese crisis is resolved by diplomacy; Germany and Japan gain control of the railways but in a manner that denies them many of its benefits. The real result is merely to ratchet up tensions and create heightened expectations in Europe and the Far East of renewed conflict.

The United States plays a major role in the China crisis, and its support for Britain and France proves decisive. Washington has strategic and economic interests in Europe and Asia but, following George Washington's advice, has remained aloof from any alliance. Successive US administrations have nevertheless drawn closer to Britain and France but are careful to go no further than public opinion will allow. Because the United States did not have the experience of World War I, no postwar reaction produces a wave of isolationism. Public opinion, especially in the heartland, is nevertheless wary of foreign involvements and consistently exaggerates the security benefits of the oceans that separate the United States from Europe and Asia.

By 1930 the United States was the world's leading economic power. In addition to its size, natural resources, and large and growing population, it has benefited from an entrepreneurial mentality, the absence of an aristocracy of birth, and low spending on defense in comparison to all other major powers. More of its money and talent go into productive enterprises and with telling effects. Europeans are impressed by US economic, scientific, and technological accomplishments but on the whole tend to regard the United States as an uncultured parvenu. Nevertheless, many Europeans feel threatened by the materialism and mass culture that political equality, economic development, and universal education have produced. This opposition is greatest among German intellectuals, steeped as they are in the Kantian idealist tradition, which scorns materialism, the give and take of democratic politics, but appreciates grand state-run and other collective projects. The German government actively encourages hostility toward the United States, France, and Britain. German officials publicize the benefits of their country's Kultur, a word better translated as *civilization* than *culture*. These officials claim Germans' collective and organic roots are the source and inspiration for German achievements in science and culture, as well as its well-ordered society. Famous German writers like Thomas Mann sign a government-sponsored letter to foreign literati expounding the superiority of German culture.

The political cold war between the Germanic and Anglo-American populations spread to culture, science, and sports. Each side steps up its efforts to excel in these domains in the hope of impressing uncommitted peoples and countries. The US Olympic Committee, racist and anti-Semitic to the core, succumbs to pressure from the White House to recruit outstanding black and Jewish athletes to help win more medals. Countries and propaganda machines on both sides encourage the defections of major public figures. Among the most prominent German defectors is Albert Einstein, who is opposed in every way to the authoritarianism and militarism of the country of his birth. Charles Lindbergh, famous for the first solo Atlantic air crossing, takes up residence in Germany, impressed by its aviation and public order and the baronetcy he receives.

The British, French, and German governments, although at peace, recognize the possibility of war, especially in light of the periodic crises that characterize their relationships. They accordingly devote considerable resources to military research and weapons development. They acknowledge Germany has an edge in naval technology, even though Britain has a larger battle fleet. The British secretly develop radar, and all the major European powers, as well as the United States, are rapidly improving their air forces. Germany and Britain investigate the possibility of jet engines, a field in which the Germans make more rapid progress. Germany begins a secret program to develop an atomic bomb, but the British and Americans quickly figure out what is up because the leading German physics journal suddenly stops carrying articles about nuclear physics. The British begin research of their own, with some voluntary American participation. Albert Einstein tries unsuccessfully to convince the US president to authorize a crash program to beat the Germans to the bomb. Once apprised of the scale of effort and cost involved, and the uncertainty of the end product, the Republican incumbent turns a deaf ear. Compulsory military service is gaining growing support in Congress, but the president promises to veto any such legislation. His standing rises several points in the polls as public opinion denies the possibility of a war in which the United States could become involved.

The German atomic program, directed by Werner Heisenberg, has gotten off to a slow start in its decision to use heavy water as a moderator in the planned reactor. But German scientists soon switch to graphite and begin refining uranium ore from Bohemia, to which they have easy access. The British program, located in Canada, uses graphite moderators from the outset. The graphite rods installed in their experimental reactors fail to conform to theoretical expectations, and considerable time elapses before scientists realize it is not as pure as the supplier has claimed. Both programs rely on gaseous diffusion to separate U235 from U238 and struggle to build centrifuges to do the job. The British effort, more than its German counterpart, suffers from the refusal of some key scientists to participate in programs designed to produce a weapon of mass destruction. Japan also begins a nuclear program but for some years does only theoretical work. Russia also becomes interested and pleads without success for its two leading scientists, Igor Kurchatov and Peter Kapitsyn, to return home from the Cavendish Laboratory in Cambridge.

The nuclear arms race, coming on top of competition in all kinds of conventional weapons development, further exacerbates tensions between the blocs. German and British military and intelligence officials now routinely engage in worst-case analysis. They readily convince themselves that their adversary is attempting to develop a first-strike capability—the ability to destroy the enemy homeland and its retaliatory weapons at the outset of any war—and would attack once it could do this. Efforts by both countries to develop long-range bombers, and rockets in the case of Germany, fuel the mutual paranoia. So does the occasional defector, some of whom find it quite profitable to fan the fears of military and intelligence officials with utterly fictional stories. Unscrupulous officials in both countries publicize their tales to frighten the public and win increased military spending. More moderate types seek to expose such fictions and restore some sanity to intelligence estimates but make little headway with the press or public opinion. Germany officials effectively silence doves with threats or preventive detention.

Growing international tensions have serious repercussions in the United States. Many Americans of German origin sympathize with their former homeland, as do those Irish Americans who hate Britain. Liberal Americans back Britain, and the business and financial communities are divided because of the high level of trade and investment with both Germany and Britain. The newly elected president, convinced that US interests would be better served by aligning with Britain, finds himself largely hamstrung by a Congress wary of authorizing military preparations that could be described as directed against either Britain or Germany.

The Prussian generals responsible for the 1918 military coup in Germany are aristocrats who want to preserve their privileges and the aristocratic order more generally. They feel threatened by socialism but also by capitalism and its material values. Field marshals Moltke and Falkenhayn think a successful war with France would weaken the Socialist party and give a big boost to the military and its more feudal values. Most German military men are less hawkish and are content with peace and their country's borders. Major industrialists are even more inclined to peace as political borders do not stand in the way of their economic penetration of eastern Europe, the Middle East, and China. The generals nevertheless realize that too long a period of peace—and Germany has been at peace since 1871—would undercut their claim to rule, based as it is on the need to maintain order and strength against foreign adversaries. Like Bismarck forty years earlier, they embrace imperialism as a means of winning the support of the middle classes. The navy—which the generals consider an expensive luxury—also serves this end as it is wildly popular and increasingly led by men of bourgeois origins. The same is true of the air force, one of whose half-Jewish pilots has made a much-publicized transpolar flight, becoming a national hero like Italo Bilbo in Italy, Blériot and St. Exupéry in France, and Lindbergh in the United States before he defects.

The generals recognize that the most effective way to maintain power is quietly. Less than a year after their coup they create a national government composed of pliant conservative politicians. This seeming return to democracy does not convince anyone, but nationalists and anti-Socialists are content with the facade. Germans go to the polls in due course, but the only candidates allowed to run for office are those who were able "to establish their national credentials." The generals use this requirement to exclude Socialists, many members of the Catholic Center Party, and anyone else with left-wing tendencies or suspected of supporting the rights or independence of ethnic minorities. A carefully managed press, preventive detention or expulsion of dissidents, and reasonable settlements with trade unions allow the regime to endure through the 1920s, 1930s, and 1940s. It is openly hostile to modern art, music, theater, and attacks of any kind on Victorian values. German culture, so vibrant before the coup, gradually dies. Intellectuals, artists, and performers of all kinds emigrate to Vienna, Paris, London, New York, or Hollywood in search of freedom and employment. To some degree this undercuts official German claims of the superiority of its Kultur, but for conservatives it reinforces those claims, as it purges the country of art and artists associated with socialism, modernism, and other political and cultural orientations anathema to the military.

Austria-Hungary is similar to Germany in many ways but more turbulent. Franz Ferdinand replaces Franz Josef as emperor in 1916 and seeks to modernize the political system and reconcile minorities, especially southern Slavs, to Austrian rule. His extension of the franchise provokes a near rebellion by Hungarians, but Germany backs Austria, and the Hungarian leaders are forced to accept political changes. Other nationalities gain greater autonomy, but at the same time the regime makes clear that it will not tolerate independence movements. The one exception is the Poles, who gain some territory to augment the Polish state created under German supervision. Nobody in Vienna is happy about this development, basically mandated by Berlin, but here too major concessions are extracted in return. An Austro-German diplomatic maneuver against Serbia compels its government to stop all nationalist propaganda against the empire or risk invasion. With German support Austria also strengthens its position in the east, making Rumania all but a satellite. As the only overt repression is against nationalists, culture and other expressions of opinion are not hindered. Anti-Semitism is rife, but individual Jews prosper, and many prominent Jewish families, like the Rothschilds, Efrussis, and Hofmannsthals, receive patents of nobility and circulate in society. Central authorities remain protective of all religious confessions and individuals who demonstrate their loyalty to the regime. Vienna, for many decades a cultural capital of world importance, becomes even more important as Berlin declines.

A COLD AND DANGEROUS PEACE

The cold war endures for decades, as did the historical Cold War between the two superpowers and their allies. In this alternative world war comes in 1975, a date chosen rather arbitrarily, but the process by which it breaks out is rooted in technological and psychological verities and has strong resonance with 1914. In both cases more responsible leaders in Vienna and Berlin would have made all the difference.

The new US president is interested in foreign policy and tries without much success to mediate the escalating conflict between the two European blocs. He also faces problems in the Pacific, where relations between the United States and Japan are tense. A serious crisis erupts over the Philippines, a former US colony that gained its independence in the 1930s but remains under Washington's heel. Tense moments occur when the Japanese fleet concentrates its forces within striking distance of the Philippines and American antiaircraft batteries protecting the island of Luzon and its important US bases shoot down a Japanese observer plane. The crisis is settled by an uneasy compromise involving some mutual concessions that American and Japanese leaders alike prefer to keep under wraps.

Britain, Germany, France, the United States, and Japan all ultimately develop and test atomic bombs. The arms race intensifies as the powers develop thermonuclear weapons and ballistic missiles to deliver them. Germany deploys nuclear submarines that within minutes of launching could destroy London and other targets in the United Kingdom and elsewhere in the empire. Britain deploys mobile ground-based missiles in France that make German targets and command-and-control centers equally vulnerable. The Continental powers invest great sums in civil defense measures, including underground shelters, but most civilians are rightfully convinced that these would not provide adequate protection. Cities lose population as people seek employment in small towns in the hope of surviving a nuclear holocaust. More and more Europeans move to Scandinavia, the United States, Canada, Australia, New Zealand, and South America, which are seen as safe havens. All these countries give priority to scientists, professionals, and skilled laborers.

Periodic war scares—some of which are outgrowths of crises, others the result of idle rumors that spread rapidly—cause panic in all European countries. They set off stampedes in which many people die as they are trampled, suffocated, or run over by motorists escaping the cities. Civil order nearly breaks down during these episodes, and governments begin to impose draconian measures. Those found responsible for rumors are prosecuted. In Germany they are executed. Even Londoners overreact, as they did during the early days of the Blitzkrieg in World War II; the famous stiff upper lip and sangfroid were the creation of wartime propagandists. The British government is compelled to impose the equivalent of wartime censorship. Although it is peacetime, countries expel or place under preventive detention many opponents of arms buildups and of restrictions on other liberties such as travel.

The European economies suffer grievously. In the better world everyone benefits from free trade and freer movement of capital, people, and ideas. Such openness is incompatible with acute political tensions among rival great powers. While some cross-bloc trade exists, all the powers give preference to their colonies and allies, primarily for strategic reasons but also because they are considered trustworthy. This insularity constrains economic opportunities and slows growth. It makes individual great powers somewhat more immune to the consequences of booms and recessions in adversarial states but also makes it more difficult for any to escape their own recessions. Extraordinary spending on defense and the brain drain of talent from Europe also hamper development. People for the most part make ends meet but live constrained, tense, and increasingly unhappy lives. High levels of anxiety lead to a significant increase in all the usual social pathologies. For the time being, Europe avoids war, but Britain—and especially Germany—increasingly develop fear-based political cultures reminiscent of George Orwell's 1984.

In this variant of my narrative even a cold peace is impossible to sustain. War comes about as the result of a series of crises that convince leaders on all sides that war is imminent, if not inevitable. Their fears become self-fulfilling. This mentality develops during the decades of an escalating cold war and despite the successive but always fruitless efforts to resolve the issues dividing the German bloc from Britain and France. The Americans sponsor repeated arms control initiatives but make little headway. In the historical Cold War negotiations among the superpowers parties were always difficult for foreign policy and domestic reasons. In our counterfactual world five powers have nuclear capability: Germany, France, Britain, the United States, and Japan. Each has different goals and different domestic constituencies with which to contend; meaningful arms control is impossible because all would have to sign off on any agreement. In the absence of arms control and any meaningful détente, the cold war remains relatively intense, although fears of war through sneak attacks decline over time. Successive crises seem to have taught British, French, and German leaders that their adversaries are as eager to avoid war as they are. This realization constitutes an informal source of reassurance, but it also constitutes a problem.

Our counterfactual cold war between the Entente Cordiale and the Central Powers periodically flares up. This happens in the 1940s and again in the late 1960s, on both occasions as a result of initiatives by aggressive German leaders. The 1960s witness several acute crises that convince many Europeans that war is more likely than at any time in the last thirty years.

The crisis spiral begins in Asia, where several colonial powers claim uninhabitable islands in the South China Sea because they sit astride rich underwater oil deposits. Periodic jockeying for position leads to the first casualties when a German destroyer fires on and kills a score of French marines, sent from Vietnam to occupy one of these rocky outcrops. The crisis is resolved when Berlin apologizes and offers compensation to the families of the dead. Not long afterward, Britain and Germany are at loggerheads over an attempted coup in Persia, a country in which Britain has considerable influence and controls most of the oilfields—as it did in the historical world. London claims that German agents arranged the assassination of Persia's pro-British premier and would have replaced him with someone beholden to them if security forces had not quickly arrested a score of conspirators and quashed the coup. Berlin denies any involvement. Britain and Germany clash again, this time about Antarctica, where German planes have dropped German flags by parachute to stake out territory claimed by Berlin. The venture is widely reported and supported in Germany. Britain and the United States are leading a campaign, opposed by Germany, Argentina, and Chile, to have the Arctic Ocean and Antarctic continent recognized as the common heritage of humanity. The event is insignificant, but Britain shows its displeasure by refusing German support ships the right to resupply at ports in South Georgia or the Falkland Islands. Germany responds, claiming labor difficulties, by closing several docks routinely used by British merchant ships in Hamburg. The tit-for-tat escalation would have continued had Washington not intervened and through quiet diplomacy convinced both countries to back down.

Far more serious is the forward deployment of German armor in Schleswig-Holstein. This is part of a campaign to bring pressure on Denmark to deny the British navy free passage into the Baltic Sea. London maintains that the Øresund is an international waterway and long recognized as such. Berlin replies that many international waterways, including the Dardanelles, have restrictions on military vessels. The Royal Navy sends several destroyers through the strait and into the Baltic to make its point. At the invitation of the Danish government, which is eager to draw closer to Britain in response to German threats, these destroyers are invited to make a port visit in Copenhagen. Berlin is outraged and sends a force to occupy one of the Frisian Islands, which are claimed by Germany but long occupied by Denmark. The Germans also send an armored regiment across the border to occupy the town of Tonder, a well-known transit point for the smuggling of opposition newspapers and propaganda into Germany. Neutral Sweden tries without success to bring about a diplomatic settlement. Berlin refuses to withdraw its force until Denmark closes the Øresund to British military traffic or London promises to abstain from sending warships into the Baltic. The crisis remains unresolved, and Britain leaks word to reporters that the admiralty is considering closing the English Channel to German shipping.

When war comes, it is accidental, not deliberate. All the nuclear powers have instituted different forms of command and control. These systems are designed to guarantee the ability to launch a retaliatory strike but also to protect against the accidental or unauthorized launch of any nuclear-tipped delivery system. The British keep their weapons unarmed. Their delivery systems are controlled by the military services, but their nuclear warheads are in the hands of a special organization created for this purpose. To marry warheads to missiles or attack aircraft, both organizations have to receive authorization through separate chains of command that come together only in the cabinet office. The Germans keep their warheads on their missiles, attack aircraft, and submarines. Security is provided by codes that have to be punched in nearly simultaneously by different officers. Both sides keep aloft rotating groups of military and political officials with the authority to launch retaliatory attacks if London or Berlin and their respective governments are obliterated in the opening moments of a nuclear exchange. This protection against decapitation, while essential, does little to reassure either government or their populations. Leaders on both sides know that the only kind of retaliation that can be ordered from these aircraft is total, removing any possibility of a limited war or a negotiated settlement.

Britain, Germany, and France use radar, signals, intelligence, and spies to monitor adversary nuclear forces. Each country implements a variety of simulation exercises designed to train operators of early warning systems and intelligence analysts to respond effectively to warnings of attack and to avoid misjudgments and panic. At the height of the Danish crisis, a training tape is somehow fed into an active channel of the British early warning system and alerts Whitehall that some German land-based missiles are preparing to attack. The system instantly alerts the prime minister; defense chiefs urge him to launch preemptive strikes against the batteries in question, which are located on the north German plain. The German missiles clearly are targeting the British task force conducting exercises in the North Sea, sent there to signal support for Denmark. A peacefully inclined fellow, dragged from his postprandial nap and horrified at the prospect of war, the prime minister wants to wait for more evidence. He insists on independent confirmation of an imminent attack. In return he agrees to order aloft the two squadrons on ready status and send them toward their point of no return. Because the tape was realistic in all features of its simulation, when additional information arrives, it includes a report confirming that one German battery has just launched its missiles.

In the interim, efforts to reach the German prime minister and general staff by telephone are unsuccessful; earlier in the crisis they evacuated to an underground command site in the Harz Mountains. The British military and foreign office crisis centers are able to reach only their counterparts, who deny any intention of attacking the task force and insist all missile batteries in north Germany had stood down days earlier to avoid raising tensions any further. This last claim seems wrong on the face of it, given the intelligence that is flowing into White-hall from the early warning center. German disclaimers are read as dis-information and more evidence that an attack is underway. Accordingly, squadron commanders, hovering at the point of no return, receive the attack order. Their movements have been picked up by German radar, and fighters are scrambled to intercept them. The British prime min-ister, defense chiefs, and their staffs are rushed to the parade ground behind Whitehall for evacuation by helicopter to an undisclosed secure command center in Wales.

As they lower their heads and run toward the waiting choppers, word arrives that all the warnings were false, prompted by a training tape. The prime minister cancels the attack but is informed the air-craft have already passed their point of no return. Standard procedure is for them to now ignore any orders on the supposition that they might originate from the enemy.

Three minutes later RAF fighters flying cover and engaged in dog-fights with German interceptors observe a cluster of mushroom clouds. One of the surviving attack aircraft reports that the two German mis-sile batteries have been destroyed. In the interim British authorities are talking to Berlin to report the grievous error they have made. The Ger-man crisis center had already alerted the kaiser and general staff about the earlier call from London. Now they are informed that British attack aircraft and fighters are entering German air space. Word soon reaches German leaders that their country is under nuclear attack.

The German prime minister thinks it strange that such an attack is seemingly limited to a few sites in the north and wants more infor-mation before authorizing any reprisal. He is a weak man, which is why he was acceptable to the generals. They quickly pressure him into launching a retaliatory strike against the British task force in the North Sea. German aircraft and U-boats trailing the ships conduct a coordinated attack with missiles and nuclear-tipped torpedoes.

The order to attack the task force goes out just as the telephone call from the British prime minister is patched through to the Harz Mountain redoubt. Now the Germans express incredulity. The general staff, listening in on the conversation between the two leaders, find the British prime minister's story of overreacting to a training tape utterly implausible and a blatant attempt at disinformation. They point out to the kaiser and German prime minister something they already knew: the British leader is a notoriously slippery politician fond of telling stories to the press and public to cover up his mistakes and those of his subordinates and to advance his political agenda. The Germans conclude that a massive attack against them is now imminent and order their forces to the highest state of readiness in order to respond to any further sign of attack.

They do not have to wait long. British aircraft report the nuclear attacks on the North Sea task force, and the British fire missiles against military airfields in the eastern and northern sectors of Germany and, as a form of retaliation, against German ships and their support facilities at the Kiel naval base. Warnings that numerous missiles and aircraft are heading their way prompt release of German missiles against British military bases and fleet units as far afield as Gibraltar. The Germans do not exempt London from their attacks but target only military command centers. The prime minister and his entourage escape London before any missiles struck and are able to order their own massive retaliation against Germany. In the immediate aftermath of these nuclear exchanges, ten million people are killed outright by heat, shockwave, and radiation. People in cities also die from falling debris, shards of glass, traffic accidents, and fires. A roughly equivalent number die sub-sequently from radiation, disease, and the effects of the breakdown of civil order, the health care system, the water supply, banking, transpor-tation, and the food chain. Dysentery, typhoid, typhus, and cholera become widespread and often fatal because of the lack of antibiotics and clean water. Parts of London and Berlin, the cities hardest hit, are transformed into black, radiating ruins.

British and German leaders quickly agree on a cease-fire but can-not turn the clock back. In less than an hour the two leading coun-tries of Europe inflicted almost unimaginable levels of destruction on themselves and nearby countries. France was the target of almost one hundred German missiles and other nuclear weapons launched from aircraft because French forces, while not integrated with those of Brit-ain, operated in tandem with them. The Germans also destroyed key Belgian and Dutch ports that the British might have used in any land war. The British in turn struck at German and allied military assets in Austria-Hungary, Poland, and Italy. Russia escaped any damage—fallout aside—and soon would use its advantage to reimpose its rule on Ukraine and suppress a subsequent bloody uprising against its occupa-tion forces. Russia is not strong enough to attack Poland but begins to exert considerable pressure on it and the Baltic states to follow its lead in foreign policy. It seems only a matter of time before they become informally incorporated into an expanding Russian bloc.

In Asia a militaristic Japan maintains strong forces in Korea and Taiwan and steps up its pressure on China to grant further trade con-cessions. It would have done the same with British, French, and Dutch colonies in the Pacific if not for Washington's immediate public com-mitment to defend them. The cold war between Japan and the United States intensifies.

THE BRIGHTER SIDE

Is anything about this world positive? The best thing about it might be what did not happen. The two world wars—and arguably the Maoist regime in China—killed more people than the Anglo-German nuclear war. Although this world has seen considerable ethnic violence in eastern Europe and the Near East, neither the Armenians nor the Jews suffer genocide, and postindependence ethnic cleansing does not occur in Africa or the Indian subcontinent. Nor does Cambodia have to endure a murderous Pol Pot regime.

In the real world the Turks routinely carried out massacres of Armenians, notably in 1894–96 and 1909. The pashas ordered the genocide in 1915 as a desperate and largely unnecessary measure to guarantee Turkey's eastern flank during World War I. Turkey's leaders would not have felt such pressure in the absence of a war, although tensions would have risen in the east if Russian Armenians had successfully declared their independence during Russia's 1918–21 civil war. As a means of checking the power of their traditional Russian enemy, the Turks might have cultivated good relations with the newly independent state of Russian Armenians.

The Holocaust was Hitler's project. Most of his generals were accomplices in the sense that they did not interfere with the SS divisions charged with carrying it out. On the eastern front some military units actively participated in the murder of Jews. German generals were military professionals, and most were interested in politics only so far as it affected their funding, manpower, and freedom from civilian control. The majority of the officer corps, but by no means all of it, was anti-Semitic, but even those who disliked Jews for the most part had no anti-Jewish agenda. Germany's Jews would have continued much as before, with the regime supporting German businessmen and scientists to serve its economic and military ends.

Russia is much better off than it was in the real world. Although subject to revolution and civil war, it escapes Bolshevism and the catastrophe of forced collectivization, the ensuing famine, purges, and World War II. Its weak democratic and then authoritarian regime is unpleasant, corrupt, arbitrary, and repressive but nothing like Stalinism. Most Russians, and citizens of other nationalities, live better, more affluent, and longer lives. More than 40 million people do not die, as they did historically, from violence or famine.

The United States and Canada are untouched by nuclear war, much to their relief. However, both suffer serious economic recessions in the aftermath of the nuclear war, as does the rest of the world because of the loss of European markets. Both countries have also benefited from avoiding two world wars in this counterfactual world. Peace is a mixed blessing for the United States economically. On the positive side it has no European debts from the First World War to write off, no Lend-Lease or Marshall Plan, and no Cold War with its extraordinary levels of unproductive defense spending and foreign military aid. More money, public and private, is invested in infrastructure and productive enterprises.

World War I made the United States the world's largest creditor nation and the dollar the world's reserve currency. World War II put the United States in the forefront of nations, a position it exploited quite single-mindedly to the advantage of its corporations and banks. Absent these wars, the United States would have been the world's largest economy but not an economic hegemon. Like all developed economies, the United States suffered through the Great Depression of the 1930s and overcame it only through wartime production. We can never know whether the Great Depression, or something like it, would have occurred in the absence of World War I and its economic and political consequences. If it did, it seems likely it would have lasted longer because any pump priming of the economy would not have been possible politically in the United States, and it would have had no need for war production in the 1940s. The United States depended less on trade than any other developed economy, but it still would have been hurt by the relative absence of free trade as the European empires in our counterfactual world retained or instituted trade preferences and barriers to protect their markets for competition from less expensive US goods and agricultural products.

The counterfactual worst world that avoids nuclear war—at least so far—is still a pretty grim place politically, economically, and culturally. People prosper economically but to a lesser extent than they do in the real world. Economic development is just as likely to occur with corporatist regimes as it is with laissez-faire capitalism. The problem is authoritarianism. Economic development benefits from more equal distribution of wealth, something made possible in much of the historical Western world by the rise of trade unions. Employers everywhere consider it in their interest to pay their workers as little as possible. Most of those who must make concessions to trade unions gripe about their labor costs. From society's perspective unions are an important, perhaps essential, engine of economic growth because they win a larger share of profits for workers. Richer workers generate more demand, creating larger markets for goods and services. In both versions of my worst world German and Japanese authoritarian regimes are responsive to demands from industrialists to suppress unions and deny workers the right to strike and engage in collective bargaining. By doing so the German and Japanese regimes damage their economies in the long term by keeping workers poor and making them resentful and less productive.

The darker scenario that results in a nuclear war has even less to recommend it. It looks good only in comparison to another counterfactual: an all-out nuclear war between the superpowers at the height of the cold war. Such a war would have killed more than a billion people, and perhaps everyone, if predictions of a nuclear winter came to pass and debris clouds so darkened the sky that crops everywhere failed.

The only way to think more positively about our worst-case scenario is to construct an upbeat aftermath to postnuclear exchange that leads to a much better world. This may seem far-fetched but so too would a narrative presented to Europeans in 1945 about how their continent would become peaceful, prosperous, and economically integrated by the end of the century. This unexpected outcome was the result of learning from the horrible events of the 1930s and 1940s and the commitment of several generations of Europeans to escaping the conflicts of the past. The massive infusion of postwar redevelopment aid from the United States also made this outcome possible. Learning and American aid might have been equally present in our postwar counterfactual world and for much the same reasons. My story ends here, yet I cannot refrain from wondering whether scholars in this reconstructed and more democratic world might speculate that Europe's nuclear war could have been prevented by minimally tweaking counterfactuals. And, if so, could the better world in which they live have come about by some other means, say, a conventional war early in the twentieth century that taught Europeans the same lessons but sooner and with less destruction and loss of life?

6

Lives in the Worst World

BOTH WORLDS THAT I DESCRIBE IN CHAPTER 5 ARE UN-pleasant for most of their inhabitants. This is true on a global scale, but the difference between Europe and North America is big. North Americans prosper, avoid war, trade with both European blocs and Japan, and spend less in absolute and relative terms on armaments than the other great powers. African Americans and Native Americans are nevertheless excluded from many, if not most, benefits of American life, and women from all backgrounds are denied the freedom and opportunities they possess in the historical world. Ethnic minorities fare a little better but still face serious barriers to professional advancement. Dorothy Parker, Claire Booth Luce, Billie Holiday, Dizzy Gillespie, Ralph Bunche, Irving R. Levine, Arthur Ashe, Harry Belafonte, Colin Powell, Mario Cuomo, Olympia Snowe, Germaine Greer, Geraldine Ferraro, and Nancy Pelosi are among the many prominent figures unknown to the general public in these worlds.

Europeans are relatively well off but not nearly as rich as they are today. Eastern Europeans have not suffered through fifty years of deprivation under Communism. Most Germans and eastern Europeans are nevertheless subject to authoritarian rule that severely constrains their freedom of political, social, and cultural expression. Italy and Austria-Hungary allow more freedom than other authoritarian governments but like their counterparts propound conservative values and Victorian attitudes toward women. In the darker of the two scenarios, large numbers of western and central Europeans lose their lives in a nuclear exchange and its aftermath.

To make comparison more meaningful, I begin with biographies of some of the same people I discussed in Chapter 4. Many are prominent in the real word and the first better world. Notable exceptions are leading Bolsheviks, who are killed, imprisoned, or forced into exile when their coup fails, and Hitler, who never has a political career. Others, who achieve fame in both worlds, live much longer. In the better world, the poets Rupert Brooke, Isaac Rosenberg, and Wilfred Owen and the artists Gustav Klimt and Egon Schiele live to a ripe old age because there is no World War I. Still other historical figures achieve renown for somewhat different accomplishments in the better world. The British economist John Maynard Keynes, to cite one example, has a different trajectory in the absence of two world wars. He does not write *The Economic Consequences of the Peace,* his best-selling 1919 book about the expected economic costs of the Treaty of Versailles. Nor is he sent to Washington to negotiate Britain's post–World War II relationship with the United States. Keynes nevertheless becomes famous for his economic writings, advises the British government on how to overcome recessions, and still ends up as master of King's College, Cambridge.

In the worse counterfactual worlds, many historical figures are prominent, but because the political and economic contexts are so different, they gain fame or notoriety in different ways or for somewhat different reasons. I offer Winston Churchill, Henry Kissinger, Barack Obama, Michael Curtiz, Humphrey Bogart, and the Freud family as examples. Many other people, prominent in the historical and better worlds, are unknown in the worse worlds. As in my better world, these worse worlds give rise to their own casts of characters.

LIVES OF POLITICAL LEADERS

Winston Churchill was among the most colorful and best known of twentieth-century world leaders. In the better world, he has an equally long and distinguished career but not as a world leader. He is famously associated with reforms intended to benefit the working class but also gains notoriety for his reactionary commitment to keeping India and other colonies British and his willingness to use violence against demonstrators. In the worse worlds his domestic commitments are unchanged in the first two decades of the twentieth century, but his colonial policy is quite different. Throughout his career Churchill was sensitive to the German threat, and he warned about the possibility of German aggression before both world wars. He does the same in the worse worlds, especially after the 1920 German military coup against the parliament and its supporters. He excoriates all British politicians who seek to accommodate Germany and who believe, naively in his view, that some modus vivendi can be achieved.

In the 1930s he becomes an embarrassment to the Tory government when he suggests that British security is being shortchanged for domestic political reasons. The government also resents his vocal support for more Indian autonomy. As the German threat intensifies throughout the 1920s and 1930s, Churchill believes it essential to wind down conflicts elsewhere. He favors home rule, even independence, for Ireland, dominion status for India, and more autonomy for mature colonies like Malaya, Hong Kong, and Egypt. These political changes, he insists, will go a long way toward accommodating indigenous elites and will reconcile them to remaining part of the British Empire. Good relations with the colonies will guarantee access to critical resources, protect the sea lanes of communication, and free ground and naval forces for use in a European war, if it comes. This position is largely anathema to the Tories and brings Churchill closer to the Labour Party, which opposes colonialism on economic and humanitarian grounds. Many Labour leaders and trade unionists are also hostile to Germany because of its suppression of workers and unions.

In 1932 Churchill shocks his parliamentary colleagues a second time by crossing the floor to join the Labour Party. When Labourites win the next election, he becomes colonial secretary and negotiates dominion status for India. He rejects all demands to create a separate Muslim political unit and uses the Indian army to suppress violence between Hindus and Muslims. Together with his Indian counterpart, Jawaharlal Nehru, he shares the 1936 Nobel Peace Prize. By then he is secretary of state for war and responds favorably to requests from leading scientists to authorize a secret program to develop atomic weapons, lest Britain be at the mercy of Germany. The British Left comes to regard him as a war criminal for creating the arsenal that nearly destroys western Europe.

Germany witnesses a succession of uninspired, faceless, and pliable prime ministers following the military coup. This situation is all but unavoidable, as the occupant of this office has to be acceptable to the general staff, not merely the Reichstag. Occasionally a colorful or talented individual emerges in a subordinate position. Among the most interesting public intellectuals is the historian Heinz Alfred

Kissinger, born in Fürth in 1923. He runs a foreign policy institute in Berlin affiliated with Humboldt University. He garners much publicity, attributable to a mix of skill and good fortune; one of his soccer team-mates—as a youth, Heinz played on local and then regional teams—is now editor of a major Berlin newspaper. Kissinger's postdoctoral thesis was on the Congress of Vienna and the Concert of Powers to which it gave rise. He praised the efforts of the three reactionary monarchies of the day—Prussia, Austria, and Russia—to maintain internal order and international peace by suppressing democratic and nationalist movements. Published commercially with a secret government subvention to lower its price, it sold well and made Kissinger a nationally known public intellectual. He continued to cultivate his relationships with policymakers and anyone else influential. He becomes an unofficial adviser, and later secretary, to the general staff, the key foreign affairs and defense body in Germany.

Kissinger is tactically brilliant, the way Bismarck was, but Kissinger, unlike his role model, is strategically unsophisticated, even misguided. His ambition is to strengthen Germany and Austria's position in Europe by breaking Russia loose from its tacit alignment with Britain and France and winning it over to the Central Powers. Such a project is quintessential Realpolitik and in Germany's interest—but not if it makes war more likely by arousing the fears of France and Britain and making them willing to risk war out of fear that the balance of power is about to shift decisively against them.

With the backing of the general staff, Kissinger makes several secret trips to Russia to meet the country's leaders in the hope of negotiating a rapprochement. He holds out the prospect of a quid pro quo: Berlin would support St. Petersburg's efforts to regain lost territory in the Caucasus, and both countries would invade Ukraine and divide it.

Russia would enter into a defensive alliance with Germany and Austria and sell most of its raw materials to them rather than to the West. Germany and Austria would be greatly strengthened and France and Britain further isolated from the Continent.

Although this protocol is secret, word leaks while negotiations are underway. The leak is presumed to be the work of Russian officials opposed to Germany and Austria. Ukrainian leaders, increasingly resentful of German attempts at domination, plead unsuccessfully with France and Britain for a defensive alliance. Charge and countercharge fly between the two blocs. Britain and France promise to increase their defense spending, and Britain hints that it might be receptive to Japanese overtures for an understanding directed against Russia, something the United Kingdom has consistently spurned in the past. Germany threatens to shift more forces toward the west, where they will threaten France, and to deploy recently perfected rocket launchers that could be targeted against British and French cities.

The crisis is not so much resolved as it dies down because neither side carries out its threats out of fear of war. Most important, Russia signs no treaty with Germany, nor does Britain with Japan. Ukraine does not come under attack, and neither bloc effects a new military buildup. Mutual restraint is nevertheless not the same as reassurance, and suspicions remain high on all sides. In another move that signals commitment to the status quo, Kissinger is eased out of his position on the general staff on the grounds that he needs more time to research his next book. Someone in authority arranges a fellowship for him at Harvard.

The United States remains aloof from all European crises, but its leaders nevertheless seek influence commensurate with their country's standing as the world's greatest economic power. Several American presidents attempt to mediate conflicts between the opposing European blocs without notable success. German and Austrian leaders distrust the United States, which despite its proclaimed neutrality they consider a strong tacit supporter of Britain and France. Paris and London welcome US support when it is forthcoming but are resentful of Washington's refusal to commit itself to defending them, although doing so is in America's economic and political interests. American leaders continually stymie efforts by Britain and France to create a league of democracy. From the perspective of Britain and France, the United States is a free rider, busy making money while others safeguard its security. The United States regularly ignores efforts of Britain and France to convince Washington to increase its defense spending. Successive agreements with administrations of both parties to upgrade defense capabilities—which also involves the purchase of European weapons systems—die in congressional committees. The British and French are convinced this is a clever ploy, abetted by American presidents, to avoid the issue.

The Kennedy family is prominent in this world although less successful in politics because of hostility to Catholicism and correspondingly greater reluctance to vote Catholics into high office. This prejudice is fueled by the existence of blatantly corrupt Catholic Democratic political machines in many cities, among them Boston, Providence, New Haven, New York, Philadelphia, Chicago, and St. Louis. Joe Kennedy Jr. is as honest as any Harvard-educated Protestant and exudes a dapper, sophisticated, and virile aura unlike the usual machine politicians. He nevertheless has good relations with local ward heelers and benefits from the service of his maternal grandfather, John "Honey Fitz" Fitzgerald, a three-term mayor of Boston. He is also known as a founding member of the Royal Rooters, early fanatical fans of the Boston

Red Sox, who for a while had the right to throw out the first ball of the season.

Joe makes a name for himself in Boston through volunteer activities and using a variety of connections to raise money for various charitable activities. He is a delegate to the 1940 Democratic Convention and wins election to Congress in 1946, where he manages to secure a seat on the transportation committee. He is enamored of aircraft, learns to fly, and holds a reserve commission in the Army Air Force. Joe works hard to build support for legislation that would fund more airports and a more effective national aviation authority. In 1952 he wins election to the Senate, and his younger brother John (Jack) replaces him in the House. The third brother, Robert (Bobby), also aspires to a political career and works in the Justice Department, where his outspoken support for civil rights antagonizes many colleagues. The youngest brother, Edward (Teddy), attends Harvard—as did his three older brothers—and graduates in 1956. He excelled in football and in 1955 caught Harvard's only touchdown pass in the Harvard–Yale game. The Green Bay Packers recruit him.

Joe is a more active senator than many and respected by his peers. He is popular in Massachusetts and develops a name for himself throughout New England. The Democratic Party is on the lookout for a vibrant, accomplished, and young face to run as vice president, and party leaders, all of whom like Joe, lament that his Catholicism disqualifies him. The Democrats had learned this lesson with the nomination of Al Smith in 1928 and are not about to repeat the mistake in a year when the Oval Office is within their grasp. The highest position to which Joe can aspire is a cabinet post in a Democratic administration, which he achieves in 1956. Jack follows his older brother's career with interest and is greatly dismayed by the virulence of anti-Catholic prejudice in the American heartland.

Let us move forward two generations to another well-known political figure: Barack Hussein Obama. He is born in Honolulu, a fact never questioned in this fictional world. Hawaii is the most tolerant state in the union on so-called racial matters, and young Barack socializes easily and is well liked by his peers from all backgrounds. He is highly intelligent, and his teachers encourage him to prepare for college and a professional career. In the second year of high school he becomes more aware of race, largely in response to reading about civil rights struggles on the mainland. He self-identifies as black, although he continues to socialize across racial and class lines. After college he wins a fellowship to Harvard Law School, where he excels academically and becomes an editor of the famous *Harvard Law Review*. He accepts a position at the University of Chicago Law School and is active in local politics. Barack is torn between his academic and political interests and recognizes that he must make a choice. He opts for a political career and wins election to Congress from the South Side of Chicago.

Obama is one of a small number of black representatives, almost all from predominantly black urban neighborhoods. They are liberal Democrats, and their party largely ignores them, taking their votes for granted. They are frustrated in their efforts to secure either legislation or executive action that would improve the living conditions and educational and economic opportunities of their constituents. Obama nevertheless makes a name for himself as an attractive and articulate politician who has easy relations with his white colleagues. He makes an unsuccessful bid for a Senate seat that is up for grabs because the incumbent has been arraigned on criminal charges, but Obama narrowly loses the primary. Public opinion polls indicate that race was the decisive factor. A frustrated but not surprised Obama accepts a professorship at the University of Hawaii Law School. During the next decade he becomes a major public figure in the state, builds a strong political base, and is elected governor in 2008. He serves two highly successful terms, and his single-payer health-care plan is widely hailed as a model for other states to emulate, although few do.

Obama becomes well known for his uncompromising position on an altogether different issue. The US-Japanese cold war began in the 1940s and never went away. In the 1990s, in response to a war-threatening crisis and fears of Japanese spying, many demanded the expulsion or roundup of people of Japanese heritage. California and Hawaii are the states with the largest populations of Japanese descent. California has a Democratic governor but an unpopular one, vulnerable to pressure from any direction. Following a riot in Los Angeles, where Japanese and Japanese Americans are attacked and two are killed, the Republican president announces that people of Japanese descent have thirty days to leave the country. Those with legal residence—today's green cards—may remain but will have to report for transport to detention camps until tensions subside. Obama, Hawaii's governor, criticizes expulsion and detention as gross overreactions and calls upon the administration to make public any evidence it has of a security threat posed by Japanese residents or Japanese Americans. The attorney general refuses to do this on the grounds of national security and does not respond to Obama's request that he be briefed on camera.

Washington orders Obama to provide the addresses of Japanese Americans and residents to the army; Obama, who has been in touch with Japanese Americans and various civic leaders, sets his counterplan in motion. Japanese Americans and residents are invited to turn themselves in, take up residence in resort hotels along Oahu's Waikiki

Beach, and limit their movement to Waikiki and Honolulu's immediate downtown. Other civic groups organize a "Parade of Freedom," in which citizens of diverse ancestry peacefully demonstrate their support for the US Constitution and its guarantees against detention without being charged with a crime and brought to a speedy trial before a jury of one's peers. A small counterdemonstration materializes, but the marches make clear that public opinion overwhelmingly supports the governor. The Japanese government is furious with Washington and privately threatens to expel all Americans from Japan. Then the Japanese arrest a prominent American businessman and his wife, accusing both of spying. The Japanese government gives evidence of the couple's activities to the press, and the American media are divided as to whether the couple are spies or have been set up.

What really inflames the White House is Obama's insistence that the federal government foot the bill for room and board at resort hotels for Japanese Americans. The president considers calling up the Hawaii National Guard and using it and the army to clear the hotels and move the Japanese Americans to the detention camp the army has set up. Students, religious leaders, and other citizens hold round-the-clock vigils at all the hotels, and any military action would involve arresting them and further alienating the state's population. This forces the White House to back down and negotiate a compromise agreement whereby Japanese tourists and expats will quietly be repatriated and Japanese immigrants allowed to return to their homes in Hawaii. Militarily sensitive areas in the state are declared off-limits to them. Governor Obama makes a conciliatory speech, and life gradually returns to normal. Relations with Japan improve, and in the interim none of its citizens is arrested and charged with a crime.

GARBO, BOGIE, AND CAFE LIFE

Back in Europe, political conflicts and periodic war scares from the 1920s to the 1950s cast a long shadow over entertainment and culture more generally. Germany loses many of its most creative artists because they are opposed to authoritarianism and unwilling to work within the narrow conservative confines set by military-appointed censors. These artists relocate to Vienna, Paris, London, and Hollywood. The German film industry never amounts to much as most actors and directors move to California.

Austria-Hungary remains a more liberal culture despite its conservative, monarchial government. Anti-Semitism is rife but not supported by the empire itself, which continues its traditional policy of welcoming and protecting groups and individuals who demonstrate their support for the state. The empire's political elite are dimly aware that Jews are the only group that identify almost fully as Austro-Hungarians. Everyone else gives primacy to some national identity.

Democratic reforms are essential to maintain legitimacy and have the greatest payoff in local government, where demagogues occasionally win office. Viennese mayor Kurt Lueger pioneers this strategy at the end of the nineteenth century, when he appealed to anti-Semites for votes, although he behaves cautiously once in office. In 1923 in the counterfactual worst world, the wholesale greengrocer Tibor Nemes runs for mayor of Budapest and wins, and the postelection celebration turns into a quasi-pogrom in which Jewish shops and a synagogue are attacked and burned. Some police shamelessly stand by and watch the mob. The outgoing mayor calls in the army to patrol the streets and protect Jewish shops and institutions. Some Jews emigrate in the aftermath, but most find reassurance in Emperor Franz Ferdinand's visit to Budapest and lunch with prominent Jews from all walks of life. The emperor's well-publicized speech praises the Austria-Hungary's Jews for their many contributions to its economic and cultural life.

The Hungarian film industry, which dates to 1896, prospers, and many of its productions, dubbed or subtitled, gained international renown. Laszlo Löwenstein (Peter Lorre), Alexander Korda, Istvan Szabo, Béla Tarr, and Miklos Jancso become household names. Adolph Zukor, who in real life founded Paramount Studios, runs a successful studio in Budapest, where the director Mihály Kertész (who was born Manó Kaminer Kertész and becomes Michael Curtiz in Hollywood) makes a series of box office hits featuring Alexander Korda and the Berlin émigré Marlene Dietrich. Josef von Starnberg produces the blockbuster *Der blaue Engel* (The Blue Angel), based on a Heinrich Mann novel and starring Dietrich. The film is banned in the United States because of its extramarital sex. Kertész occasionally directs in Hollywood, and some studio people work in Budapest. Hollywood's money attracts Europeans, but its Victorian narrowness also repels them. American actors are drawn to Europe for its creativity and freedom, but most speak only English, and performance roles are accordingly limited.

In the historical world Curtiz is most famous as the director of *White Christmas* and *Casablanca*. The latter, iconic for at least two generations of young Americans, is never made in the counterfactual worlds. No World War II means no Nazis, Vichy France, and French resistance, and, except for the Americans Humphrey Bogart and Dooley Wilson (Sam), the other principals are Europeans who do not emigrate to America. Swedish Ingrid Bergman becomes a mainstay of the German film industry in the better world and remains in Sweden in the worse one. Paul Henreid (Victor Laszlo) was born Paul Georg Julius Henreid Ritter von Wassel-Waldingau, the son of an aristocratic

Viennese banker. Also from Austria-Hungary was Peter Lorre (Signor Ugarte), born in Ružomborek in present-day Slovakia. Claude Rains (Louis) and Sydney Greenstreet (Signor Ferrari) were English. Conrad Veidt (Major Strasser) was German. Among the minor characters, Curt Bois (the pickpocket) was German, Leonid Kinsky (Sascha) Russian, and S. Z. Sakall (Carl the waiter) Hungarian. In the real world Henreid, Veidt, Bois, and Sakall fled the Nazis and came to the United States. Most of these people pursue their careers in Europe in the better and worst worlds.

Bogart, the son of a New York surgeon, also leads a different life. Raised in a rather strict and emotionally repressed family, the young Humphrey is teased for his curls and the Little Lord Fauntleroy outfits in which his mother dresses him. She is a phenomenally successful commercial artist who uses family connections to get her son accepted at Phillips Academy in preparation for Yale. At eighteen Bogart is expelled for carousing and lack of studiousness, and in the real world he joins the navy in the last year of World War I. He is an exemplary sailor and adores Paris and its women.

Without a war a young man in search of adventure is less likely to choose a military career. Still drawn to the sea, Bogart joins the merchant marine and spends a couple of years traveling around the world and greatly enjoying the adventure. He revels in the escape from the stifling conservative atmosphere of his family and its social circle and develops liberal political views and commitments. Back in New York in 1921, he renews his friendship with his boyhood pal Bill Brady Jr., whose father has recently started his own production company, World Films. Bogart tries his hand at screenwriting and directing and finally wins several bit parts. He likes the late hours actors keep and the attention they receive, especially from women. He later tells a friend, "I was born to be indolent and this was the softest of rackets."

Bogart gradually makes a name for himself on Broadway as a serious actor. In the real world theater suffered grievously after the 1919 stock market crash, and many thespians, Bogart included, took off for Hollywood in search of employment. With no Great Depression he stays longer in New York and begins to make movies only in the mid-1930s. His Hollywood drinking buddy Spencer Tracy gets Bogart his first parts, and he goes on to star in a series of westerns. Without Peter Lorre or Sydney Greenstreet, no one makes the *Maltese Falcon* or *Casablanca*. Bogart makes a good living, but the closest he comes to stardom is as a deeply conflicted but virtuous cowboy in a John Huston allegory about small-town corruption. In real life Bogart is drawn to the classics in philosophy and history, especially to Plato and Shakespeare. In the worse counterfactual world Bogart continues to read voraciously, occasionally attends public lectures at UCLA, and becomes active in actors' efforts to unionize to counter the studios more effectively. He does some benefits on behalf of migrant farmworkers, who are also in the process of organizing, and is badly beaten up by thugs hired by grape producers to intimidate labor organizers and their supporters.

This experience makes Bogart more committed to the cause. He pulls off a complicated double cross by posing as someone willing to do a deal with the grape producers. He secretly tapes their conversation, in which his interlocutors expose themselves as greedy men responsible for violence against farmworkers. A liberal newspaper publishes the transcript, and the state legislature holds hearings that result in a big victory for the union and farmworkers. His Hollywood career ends as he is put on a secret blacklist. Bogart occasionally appears in California stage productions and gains renown for his portrayals of King Lear and Hamlet, two of his favorite characters.

Many real-world critics consider 1939 the best year in film history. Audiences were treated to the American films *The Wizard of Oz, Gone with the Wind, Ninotchka, Gunga Din, Mr. Smith Goes to Washington,* and *Goodbye, Mr. Chips.* It was also the year for the British *Jamaica Inn,* directed by Alfred Hitchcock and starring Charles Laughton and Maureen O'Hara; *The Lion Has Wings,* with Ralph Richardson and Merle Oberon; and the French *La Règle du jeu* (Rules of the Game), starring Jean Gabin, and *Le jour se lève* (Daybreak), directed by Jean Renoir. Most of the American films probably would have been made in some shape or form in the counterfactual worlds. An important exception is the exquisitely humorous *Ninotchka* because no Soviet Union or its Five Year Plan exists to parody, and no Greta Garbo is in Hollywood to play the leading lady. Charlie Chaplin would not have made *The Great Dictator* in 1940 without Hitler. He would have returned to Europe earlier than he did, given his lifestyle and antagonism to American puritanism and conservatism.

In the real autumn of 1939 the British and French film industries shifted to wartime production, as the United States would in 1942. In the counterfactual worlds World War II does not occur, so the film industries in these countries can chug merrily along, largely oblivious, especially in America, to troubling events and controversies. Hollywood is even more conservative, so John Ford could not have made a film in 1940 of John Steinbeck's novel *The Grapes of Wrath.* Henry Fonda would have had to achieve stardom through some other vehicle. War movies became a Hollywood staple, and without both world wars and the Korean War, movies would have fallen back on the Civil War, and Hollywood would have produced even more westerns.

If America is culturally confining and Hollywood positively infantilizing in the counterfactual worlds, much of continental Europe suffers worse constraints imposed by its authoritarian regimes. Only in Austria-Hungary and Italy do creative and performing artists have relatively more freedom, provided they do not advocate separatism or criticize their governments. Within strict limits government criticism is possible in Austria-Hungary. Vienna and Budapest, and other cities in the empire—most notably Prague, Pressburg (Bratislava), Krakow, Trieste, and Laibach (Ljubljana)—have orchestras and operas under the batons of Bruno Walter, Eugene Ormandy, George Szell, Fritz Reiner, Antal Doráti, and Paul Kletzki. In Italy Arturo Toscanini and Tullio Serafin rule La Scala and conduct elsewhere in Italy and Europe.

In my worst world, Vienna's coffeehouses continue to attract writers, intellectuals, and political exiles, although none on the wanted list of Russia's secret police dares show their faces. Sigmund Freud favors the Café Landtmann. Here and elsewhere Freud frequently shares a table with the writers Arthur Schnitzler and Stefan Zweig, the painter Gustav Klimt, the architect Adolf Loos, the journalist and Zionist Theodor Herzl, and Freud's fellow analyst Alfred Adler. Alma Mahler is not a cafe type, preferring to socialize in salons. In 1920 she divorces the architect Walter Gropius to marry the writer Franz Werfel, with whom she already has a son, who was born prematurely and does not survive.

Arthur Schnitzler, Robert Musil, Joseph Roth, and Franz Werfel write critically acclaimed and best-selling novels in the real and counterfactual worlds. A common theme among them is the alienated individual who feels out of place in his country, society, and even circle of friends and struggles to define himself and defend his fragile ego. This problem becomes more acute as the century progresses, and writers, not only in Austria but elsewhere, turn to mysticism, aestheticism, psychoanalysis, nationalism, and socialism in search of solutions.

Schnitzler was a member of Young Vienna (Jung Wien) and the first German to write in stream of consciousness. He was open about sexuality, and his 1900 short story *Lieutenant Gustl* offers a most unflattering portrait of army officers and their honor code. Schnitzler was stripped of his reserve commission in the medical corps. In later novels he offers biting and amusing critiques of Viennese society. Franz Werfel was born in Prague and was a contemporary and acquaintance of Franz Kafka, Max Brod, and Martin Buber. Werfel served in the Austro-Hungarian army in World War I, first on the Russian front and then in Vienna, where he met Alma Mahler. His 1929 novel, *The Forty Days of Musa Dagh,* publicized the Turkish genocide of Armenians. Werfel left Austria at the time of the Anschluss and barely made it to the United States, where he died in 1945. Hitler later condemned Werfel's works as "Jewish filth." In the worse counterfactual world, Werfel and Alma remain in Vienna, he continues to produce novels, and he never writes for Hollywood.

In the counterfactual worlds Musil and Roth are still interested in individual and national identity but approach these questions in a different way. Their great novels, *The Man Without Qualities* and *The Radetzky March,* explore life in the empire retrospectively and are set on the eve of what the authors, but not their characters, know will be the Great War, which ends with the defeat and dissolution of Austria-Hungary. By gradually stripping away all layers of social identity, Musil shows that there is no unique, independent self, only a bundle of raw appetites. Roth's novel describes three generations of the Trotta family who rise from humble origins to nobility and pretensions and concern for honor and status; their elevation brings about their downfall. The family is intended to represent the empire.

Without the war and its consequences, both authors would have regarded Austria differently. Although antiquated in structure and ruled by an aristocracy and a bureaucracy imbued with premodern values, the empire would have looked good in the 1920s and 1930s in comparison with its neighbors. It was politically and culturally freer, more socially relaxed, and more fun loving than Germany and Russia, and it was better run and less chaotic than Italy. Musil still makes identity the theme of his great novel, but it does not center on the futile search of a committee of notables to find a way of celebrating the seventieth year of Franz Josef's reign. The novel is set five years later, in 1919, and chronicles the confusion created by the reform efforts of the new emperor, Franz Ferdinand. The reforms not only arouse political opposition, especially among Hungarians, but also more generally compel people to reconsider their loyalties and the extent to which their sense of self is derived from class or national affiliations. Musil shows how shallow these identifications are, how easily they are rewritten by people to suit their current social and psychological needs, but also how essential they appear to be. He does this by removing them and describing the greater aporia that results for all the characters involved.

For Musil and Roth Austria-Hungary emerges as a unique blend of old and new whose political and social structures are entirely indefensible and most inefficient but nevertheless allow creative self-fashioning that is conducive to individual happiness and political order. This is in sharp contrast to Germany—the 900-pound gorilla in the novel and in Austria's background—where self-fashioning is destructive to individuals and order alike. Roth remains fascinated by the fictional Trotta family but adds another generation in the character of a young idealist committed to supporting political reforms and breaking out of the constraints imposed by his family and old order. Critics read this renewed support for the empire among its intellectuals into the art of Klimt and music of Mahler in the counterfactual worlds, although this requires considerable intellectual gymnastics.

RICKETY PLANES, POLIO, AND ROTARY PHONES

Science progresses at a different pace and on different fronts in my imaginary world than it does in the real world. There are two big differences. Without two world wars government provides less support for science so it develops more slowly on every front. The better world has a diminishing need for weapons, so it has no crash programs to develop atomic bombs. Treaties prohibit such weapons, and an international consortium, advised by scientists and with the right of inspection, manages nuclear energy. The worse counterfactual world has conventional and nuclear arms races, and, as in the historical world, resources and talent are directed away from productive areas of scientific inquiry and technological development and toward expensive military projects. The second difference concerns the pace of scientific development. The worse counterfactual world is more authoritarian and closed than its historical counterpart, less scientific talent is concentrated in the United States, and less American funding goes into basic research. For all these reasons scientific progress on all fronts is slower. Commercial aviation, antibiotics, and other medical innovations are delayed, as is the emergence of such fields as computer science, nanotechnology, and biotechnology.

As I previously noted, many of Europe's top talents leave for greener, more democratic pastures, notably the United Kingdom and the United States. Not only does Europe become less competitive scientifically, this problem threatens to become endemic as the next generation of students has fewer leading minds to guide their studies and research. The exodus from Europe is still a trickle in comparison to the historical world. Jews in both are overrepresented in science and culture, and fewer emigrate in the worse world because, although anti-Semitism flourishes, Hitler does not exist, and Jews face no racial laws and no threat of extermination. Remember too that the United States is far less tolerant in the worse world and does not welcome Jewish immigrants. In Europe and North America much talent is wasted.

The lives of Sheldon Glashow, Steven Weinberg, and Abdus Salam provide vivid illustrations of the differences between these worlds. Glashow, the son of Russian Jewish immigrants, was born in New York City in 1932. He shared the 1979 Nobel Prize in physics with Weinberg and Salam for their contributions to the theory of the unified weak and electromagnetic interaction among elementary particles. Weinberg was born in 1933 to Jewish parents who had fled anti-Semitism in Europe. He was in the same class as Glashow at the Bronx High School of Science, and both did their undergraduate studies at Cornell. Weinberg went on to the Bohr Institute in Copenhagen and finished his PhD at Princeton. Glashow went to Harvard, where he studied with Julian Schwinger, who made major contributions to quantum theory and won the Nobel Prize in 1965 for quantum electrodynamics. The scion of a Polish Jewish immigrant family, Schwinger went to the City College of New York (CCNY), Columbia, and finally to Berkeley, where he received his PhD under the tutelage of J. Robert Oppenheimer. Mohammed Abdus Salam, born in 1926 in a poor rural district of the Punjab, was the first Muslim and Pakistani to become a Nobel laureate in the sciences. His father wanted him to train for the civil service, but he doggedly pursued his interests in mathematics and graduated from the Government College University. He won a scholarship to St. John's College, Cambridge, where he quickly distinguished himself. He stayed in Cambridge at the Cavendish Laboratory and earned his PhD. His doctoral thesis won him instant international recognition for its contributions to quantum electrodynamics. Salam visited various American universities in the course of his career and returned to Pakistan in 1950, where he played a major role in his country's development of nuclear facilities and research.

The Bronx High School of Science was an institution open to talent regardless of background, and students gained admission on the basis of competitive examinations. Like its Budapest counterpart, it produced a string of prominent scientists, as did CCNY. The Bronx High School of Science counts seven Nobel laureates in physics and six Pulitzer Prize winners among its graduates; CCNY counts twelve Nobelists, in physics, chemistry, medicine, and economics, among its alumni. In our worse counterfactual world these achievements are less likely. The parents of Glashow and Weinberg—and of these other high achievers—would have found it correspondingly more difficult, if not impossible, to emigrate to the United States and for their sons to be accepted at Ivy League institutions. I should note that Cornell was more open to Jewish students than most, as Weinberg and Glashow recognized. Another talented individual in this situation was Hyman Rickover, who oversaw development of the world's first nuclear-powered submarine. He was born in a part of Russia that is now Poland and, as a young boy, came to Illinois with his parents and later gained admission to the US Naval Academy.

Abdus Salam's trajectory is more certain in his younger years, as Cambridge and Oxford were open to talent from the Raj. However, it is unlikely that Salam would have returned home to an independent Pakistan, and certainly no nuclear programs exist in South Asia in the counterfactual worlds. With fewer physicists from the developing world earning PhDs at European and American universities, and colonialism lasting a couple of decades longer at the very least, nuclear proliferation probably would not have extended beyond Europe, with the exception of Japan.

In the historical world Vienna was the home of psychiatry, but after the Germans occupied Austria in 1938, the locus shifted to New York. Freud fled Vienna for London in 1938, and his extended family soon followed. He was already a sick man and died the next year from throat cancer. In the worse counterfactual world, Freud remains in Vienna, and life is fundamentally unchanged, although the problem of war and the rise of the Nazis do not consume his later work. His family leads very different lives. Sigmund and Martha Bernays had six children and many grandchildren. Several had interesting, if not colorful, careers. Their oldest son, Anton Walter Freud, was a chemical engineer and during World War II served behind enemy lines in Britain's Special Operations Executive. Their youngest son, Ernst Ludwig, was a prominent architect in Berlin and London who was influenced by Ludwig Mies van der Rohe. The youngest daughter, Anna Freud, trained as a psychoanalyst and founded the field of child psychiatry with Melanie Klein.

In the real world the most famous grandchild is Lucien Michael Freud, the portrait painter whom some consider the leading British artist of his generation. Another high achiever was Clement Raphael

Freud, who was an English bon vivant, broadcaster, writer, member of Parliament, and chef. In World War II he served in the Royal Ulster Rifles and was an aide to Field Marshal Montgomery. Afterward Clement Raphael participated in the Nuremberg trials. Several great grandchildren are prominent, among them George Lowenstein, professor of economics and psychology at Carnegie Mellon University; David Anthony Freud (Baron Freud), a businessman who served as parliamentary undersecretary for work and pensions in Britain; Jane McAdam Freud, whose prints, drawings, and sculptures are widely displayed in Britain and abroad; and Esther Freud, a novelist.

Freud's children, grandchildren, and great grandchildren lead very different lives in the better and worse worlds. I do not provide fictional reconstructions of any of them but offer the Freud family as emblematic of all the Jewish and other refugees who fled the Fascists, Nazis, and Communists. They settled on the peripheries of Europe, Palestine, North and South America, and the Far East. My wife's family offers another, if less illustrious, version of this story. The few members of her once-large family who survived the Nazis were born in Austria-Hungary, escaped from what was by then Czechoslovakia, and found refuge in Palestine, Shanghai, New Zealand, and the United States, the last after a prolonged stay in Bolivia. My wife and her siblings live in Melbourne, Boston, and London. When I was growing up in Queens, my block was filled with immigrants who had left Germany, Austria, Italy, and the Soviet Union for political or religious reasons. The Germans were primarily Catholic or socialist and as anti-Nazi as their Jewish neighbors. Their kids, my friends, grew up to become civil servants, entrepreneurs, lawyers, doctors, dentists, professors, and a writer. One, who was born in the Soviet Union, became wealthy enough to buy a seat on a rocket to the Soyuz space station.

This story has numerous variations in every decade in which immigrants came to the United States in search of political freedom or economic opportunities. Between the wars it would include Ieoh Ming Pei, born in Canton in China in 1917, who arrived in the United States at eighteen to study architecture at MIT. Among his best-known buildings are the East Wing of the National Gallery of Art in Washington, DC; the John F. Kennedy Memorial Library in Boston; and the new entrance and visitor's center at the Louvre in Paris. The Taiwanese Jerry Yang came to California with his family when he was ten years old. He did his undergraduate and graduate education at Stanford, where he was cocreator of an Internet directory that later became Yahoo! The Hungarian-born Andrew Grove received his PhD in chemical engineering from Berkeley and is cofounder of Intel. Au Wang, who emigrated from Shanghai, China, in 1945, earned his PhD in applied physics from Harvard. He holds more than thirty-five patents and founded Wang computers, a pioneer in the field. The Russian-born Sergei Brin came to the United States with his parents in 1979. He earned his PhD in computer science at Stanford and founded Google with Larry Page. His personal wealth is estimated to be in the range of $20 billion.

In our real historical world, the United States benefited enormously economically, scientifically, culturally, and culinarily from immigration—and through the United States the rest of the world benefited, too. In the better world, most of these people would have stayed put, like the majority of famous people whose lives I have discussed in more detail. In the worse counterfactual world, more would have wanted to emigrate, but most would have found it much more difficult because their governments would not let them out or they would not have been welcomed abroad. The United States does not have a good record for admitting refugees from Mussolini and Hitler, but it is even more closed to immigration in the worse-world scenario. As a result Britain, Canada, and the United States are far less cosmopolitan and culturally pluralistic than they are today. Their economies and cultural lives are correspondingly impoverished.

JIM CROW

Would-be immigrants are not the only people who face much higher barriers in the worse counterfactual world. African Americans, women, and ethnic minorities are all disadvantaged. Efforts to improve their lot meet much more resistance in the worse world than they did in the historical and better worlds.

Absent two world wars, mass migration to the North, Midwest, and West by black Americans, and the subsequent movement by many of them, or their children, into the commercial and professional classes, the civil rights movement is set back by several decades. Without integration of the armed forces, public schools, and universities, many whites are much less receptive to black demands for equality. This is true in the better and worse counterfactual worlds. In Chapter 4, I looked at some consequences of discrimination for black jazz musicians, who were either compelled by circumstances or simply found it far more attractive to work and live in Europe. In this chapter I examine the lives of Jackie Robinson and Barack Obama.

The worse world is worse still for African Americans because discrimination abroad is greater and they are less welcome abroad, except in France, Holland, and Britain. The Supreme Court makes the same ruling in *Plessy v. Ferguson* (1896) as it did in the historical world, so segregation remains the law of the land. It is practiced almost everywhere, de jure or de facto, with the notable exception of Hawaii.

Black schoolchildren must attend crowded, underfunded, and often unsafe schools, and most white universities are either closed to black high school graduates or admit them in very small numbers. The larger white community largely ignores gifted black artists and intellectuals, and many must support themselves in menial jobs where they are routinely addressed as "boy" by white employers and customers. Those who refuse to accept such humiliation risk losing their jobs or, worse still in certain parts of the country, their lives. As late as 1950 the United States averages one hundred lynchings per year, and the authorities usually look the other way.

In the historical world the position of women gradually improved during the twentieth century. During World War II women entered the workforce in large numbers, and many took jobs previously thought to require the strength or other qualities usually regarded as male. In the United States Rosie the Riveter was literally the poster child for this development. After the war women were largely forced out of the labor markets in the United States and Britain, somewhat less so in Germany and the Soviet Union because of severe shortages of manpower. In the United States middle-class women were expected to be homemakers, and those in the workforce were largely restricted to professions deemed suitable to women (e.g., nursing, teaching, librarians). They were paid less for comparable responsibility and work.

The feminist movement, made possible and inspired in part by the civil rights movement, gradually improved the status of women. In the United States and Western Europe women achieved equal legal rights, professions opened up, and female sexual needs and interests became more widely recognized. In more socially advanced countries women gained the right to abortion almost on demand. By the 1970s women began to hold key political positions around the world. Prominent female leaders of that decade include Isabel Perón in Argentina, Golda Meier in Israel, Indira Gandhi in India, Maria de Lourdes Pintasilgo in Portugal, and Margaret Thatcher in the United Kingdom.

Little progress of this kind occurs in the better counterfactual world and none of it in the worse world, where attitudes toward women remain puritanical. In the better world I described the life of Athalia Fetter Kennedy, first lady in the Joseph Kennedy administration. She is compelled to give up her professional career so her husband can pursue his political one, and her outspokenness draws much criticism. In the worse counterfactual world, she becomes a model and actress but not a game show host. Many women of her generation and the next encounter similar restrictions, and only relatively small numbers of women become doctors, attorneys, professors, architects, scientists, and entrepreneurs. Women are also more socially constrained because birth control is not widely available and in some states still prohibited by law. Abortion remains strictly illegal. Neither a sexual nor social revolution occurs; in its absence American men continue to divide women into two categories: those with whom they have sex and those they marry. The former are considered sluts and the latter glorified but just as often abused.

In the United States, these values are propagated in families, schools, Hollywood, and television. TV sitcoms feature ditzy women like Lucy or those smart enough to defer to their husband's needs and wishes even when they give hints of thinking them unwise or even foolish. No roles are written for strong, decisive, career-oriented women. In the historical world *The Mary Tyler Moore Show* was a breakthrough in this connection. It aired on CBS from 1970 to 1977, and its episodes feature a single career woman in her thirties who is not engaged, divorced, or in search of a man. She has previously broken off an engagement and moved to Minneapolis, where she applied for a secretarial position at a radio station but is somehow hired as assistant producer of its *Six O'Clock News.* She is later promoted to producer. The show won praise from critics and received multiple Emmy Awards.

The success of *Mary Tyler Moore,* and the emergence of the women's movement, encouraged the networks to air other sitcoms like *Rhoda, Phyllis,* and *Maude* and adventure shows like *Police Woman* and *The Bionic Woman* that featured independent female characters. In the 1970s publications and other activities of writers and politicians like Gloria Steinem, Betty Friedan, Robin Morgan, Kate Millet, Shirley Chisholm, Elizabeth Holtzman, and Bella Abzug advanced feminism and the fight for equality. Equally important was the development of effective, inexpensive, and readily available methods of birth control and the landmark 1973 Supreme Court decision, *Roe v. Wade,* legalizing abortion. None of this happens in the worse world.

The worse world has pockets of liberalism in the United States and United Kingdom, notably in intellectual, artistic, and bohemian circles, where women find more freedom of expression. But such opportunities are generally restricted to wealthy educated white women. Most women are restricted to the role of housewife or a small number of acceptable professions where they are underpaid in comparison to their male counterparts and subordinate to them. Even talented female authors find getting published more difficult, and those that do must temper their writings to appeal to mass audiences to achieve commercial success. One of the few female authors to achieve notable critical and financial success is the Canadian writer Margaret Atwood. She was born in 1939 and started writing at an early age. In the historical world she attended the University of Toronto and did graduate studies at

Harvard. She subsequently taught at Canadian and American universities and received an honorary doctorate in Ireland. She has published novels, stories, poems, essays, and criticism and has won a number of coveted awards. Perhaps her most controversial works are her science fiction and feminist writings. *The Handmaid's Tale,* published in 1985, received the Arthur C. Clarke Award and the Governor General's Award and was short-listed for the Booker Prize. This dystopian novel is set in a United States that has become a totalitarian theocracy that subjugates women by every means possible.

No publisher will touch such a work in the worse counterfactual worlds, not even liberal science fiction magazines and book publishers. Margaret Atwood becomes a successful author but one who can only hint at the ways by which women can become empowered. She still finds the conceit of alternative worlds attractive, and her most widely read novel, *Susan's Journey,* takes place in an imaginary United States dominated by liberal values and greater equality for women. Her heroine grows up in a small Midwestern city, attends the state university, and becomes a publishing executive in New York. To gain sophistication and professional success she must break from traditional parents and a long-standing love who wants to marry her and make her a mother and homemaker. On the job she must thread a careful path through the labyrinth of office politics, where advancement for women often comes in return for sexual favors. Susan is heterosexual but has a short relationship with a woman on the rebound from several unsatisfactory, self-centered male lovers.

Susan's Journey is published in Canada and quickly banned in the United States because of its sexual content. It appeals to a young audience and, next to scotch whiskey, is the item most frequently smuggled across the border. Courts in Pennsylvania and Ohio refuse to lift the proscription against the novel, and the case is working its way up to the Supreme Court.

JACKIE AND BARACK

Sport is a largely national affair in the historical world and more so in the counterfactual worlds. To be sure, all have Olympic Games, World Cups, and Super Bowls, as well as European soccer competitions, and cricket, rugby, and field hockey matches within the British Empire. The World Series is a misnomer, as it is a purely North American contest. The most international sport is tennis, and the United States, Britain, French, and Australian opens draw competitors from around the world. Black athletes are excluded from most of these competitions because baseball, where the color barrier was broken in the historical world, remains segregated longer in both counterfactual worlds. Tennis has no black players, and few blacks even play tennis, as local clubs do not recruit and train aspiring talent. In soccer hardly any colonial athletes make professional teams in Europe, and few fans cheer efforts to place them on national teams.

In the United States continuing segregation extends the life of the Negro League beyond 1951 and into the early 1970s. A separate black basketball league also develops, as this sport also remains segregated. Both leagues, and a nascent football league, draw large audiences because of the skill of the players. Black baseball and basketball are faster games, and white sportswriters routinely comment on the superb strategic sense of their managers and players. Periodically white owners and their managers attempt to break the color barrier in baseball, beginning with Bill Veeck in 1943 and Branch Rickey in 1947. Baseball commissioner Kennesaw Mountain Landis and National League President Ford

Frick block their efforts. Happy Chandler and later commissioners are more open to integration, but team owners band together to rein in renegade owners who are eager to hire Negro players to improve the standings of their teams. A Supreme Court case in 1958, sponsored by the National Association for the Advancement of Colored People, upholds school segregation. This makes it easier to maintain the so-called gentlemen's agreements in baseball, housing, and private education.

Talented black Americans have fewer freedoms and fewer opportunities. This fact is evident in the career of Jackie Robinson, one of the most talented athletes of his generation. Born in 1919 into a family of Georgian sharecroppers, he was the youngest of five children. After being deserted by her husband, Mallie Robinson moved her family to Pasadena, California. Jackie grew up poor in an affluent white community. He was excluded from many recreational activities because of his skin color and toyed briefly with joining a gang. His two older brothers, one of whom became an Olympic medalist, encouraged him to play sports in high school, and he excelled at football, basketball, baseball, tennis, and track.

Jackie went on to Pasadena Junior College, where his athletic prowess gained wider recognition. In January 1938 he was arrested for complaining to the police about the unjustified detention of one of his friends. For his outspokenness against this act of racism he was given a two-year suspended sentence. His older brother Frank died in a motorcycle accident, and Jackie decided to continue his education at UCLA so he could be closer to his family. In 1941 he went to Hawaii to play football for the racially integrated Honolulu Bears. In the alternative world he falls in love with Hawaii, where he encountered little prejudice. He and Rachel decide it is the right place to raise their children. For six years Jackie plays semipro football in the winter season and semipro baseball in the summer. He then accepts a job as athletic director of Punahou High School in Honolulu. He finds the position satisfying as it combines athletics with mentoring students, some in need of more guidance off the playing field than on it.

In real life, Jackie died in 1972 from a combination of heart disease and diabetes. In the counterfactual worlds he is in better health because he avoids the stress associated with his role in integrating baseball. Perhaps more important for his health, his oldest son does not develop emotional problems, is not wounded in action in Vietnam, does not became a drug addict, and does not die in a car accident. One of the young men he coaches in basketball and mentors is Barack Obama. They remain in touch after Obama leaves for the mainland, and they become close friends after his return. Jackie functions as an informal adviser when Obama becomes governor, someone outside politics to whom Obama could turn for independent advice or simply use as a sounding board. Jackie helps stiffen Obama's resolve, and Obama, keen to live up to his mentor's expectations, implements his daring policy of resistance to the proposed roundup of Japanese Americans. Jackie Robinson lives until 1992, long after he retired from Punahou.

SUDDEN DEATH

The year 1972 is a turbulent one in the counterfactual United Kingdom. Miners are on strike; unemployment reaches high levels; the Irish Republican Army launches a new wave of attacks; Edward, duke of Windsor, dies; and air and rail disasters occur. Yet another polio epidemic claims the lives of thousands of young people and maims even more. John Lennon and David Cameron are two of its many victims. The race for the soccer championship is tight, won in the end by the Hotspurs, and the Glasgow Rangers win the European Cup. Agatha Christie publishes a new Hercule Poirot novel, and the West End sees a fine season of new plays. As always relations with Germany are tense, but no crisis looms.

Early October brings unusually warm weather, and those who can afford it make excuses to spend time in the country. The royal family is in residence at Balmoral, the annual apple festival is underway in Buckinghamshire, a crafts and food fair in Cheshire, the Falmouth Oyster Festival in Cornwall, and Autumn Wild Days Out in Glasgow. At universities throughout the United Kingdom the school year has just begun, and on Saturday, October 7, many students are outside enjoying the good weather.

In Cambridge three graduate fellows—two British and the third Irish—from Pembroke College are walking along the river to Grantchester to lunch at the Orchard. It is famous for its association with Rupert Brooke and the Bloomsbury Set, but foremost in the minds of the students are their expectations of lounging in its deck chairs and consuming their sandwiches with a pot of tea. As one predicted, half of Cambridge has the same idea, and they find no free seats and a long queue in the badly managed cafeteria. They leave the Orchard and follow the path through fields along the Cam looking for a decent place to picnic. They finally find one beside an old oak tree. As they remove their food from a hamper and begin to unwrap the sandwiches, a tremendous burst of light flashes twenty-nine kilometers (eighteen miles) to the northeast. A German nuclear weapon of 200 kilotons has exploded at an altitude of 2,000 feet above the Royal Air Force base at Mildenhall in Suffolk.

Everyone within several miles of ground zero is vaporized, and many more people are killed by the shockwave, which spreads out unimpeded by the flat land or much in the way of strong buildings. At the picnic site one student is instantly blinded, as he had been looking across the river in the direction of the blast. The other two, temporarily blinded, throw themselves to the ground in recognition that something horrible has happened and quickly conclude that it is an atomic blast. This is seemingly confirmed by the rise of a mushroom cloud. The blast wave, which carries 40 to 50 percent of the energy of the explosion, can travel several hundred kilometers an hour and reaches them in about ten minutes. One student, a physicist, does a rough calculation and convinces his friends that they have time to seek shelter in the Green Man pub. They do this and nurse their pints, wondering how much radiation they have absorbed. If they vomit within the hour, they learn over the radio, they have little chance of survival.

Experiences of this kind are widespread in Britain, France, and Germany. In the immediate vicinity of blasts, large numbers of people are killed instantly or die within days of radiation poisoning. Civil order and public health break down, and authorities bring in soldiers, police, health personnel, and administrators from unaffected locales to do what they can to help survivors. Telephones are useless as the circuits are quickly overloaded; everyone is trying to reach family, friends, and loved ones. The prime minister and his cabinet survive and return to London, which has been the target of multiple nuclear weapons. They inspect damage and show themselves to survivors, even at the risk of exposure to radiation. The prime minister goes on the radio—TV service is intermittent and dysfunctional in many locales—and asks listeners not to use the phones so they are available for rescue and related operations. He also pleads, with much less effect, for London residents in neighborhoods that have not sustained damage to stay put. People continue to flee in every direction but without much success as subways, buses, and train lines are down. Automobile traffic is more or less at a standstill, as many roads leading to the periphery are gridlocked, the result of desperate drivers and nonfunctioning traffic lights. After hours without moving, many people have left their cars in search of food and water, making it impossible in some cases for other vehicles to get around them. Hospitals are overflowing and short of staff because personnel cannot travel from home to hospital. Ambulances are all but useless on London's impassable roads. Many survivors reluctantly begin to envy those who were vaporized and died without pain or knowledge of what was happening to them.

7

Looking Back at the Real World

ALL WORLDS AND EVENTS CAN BE EVALUATED ON THE BA-
sis of their contingency. At one extreme we encounter the butterfly effect, where a small change has the potential to generate a vastly different
future. Edward Lorenz, who coined the term, suggests that a butterfly
flapping its wings somewhere in Central America might alter air cur-
rents in a way that causes them to build up and ultimately give rise to a
hurricane that would not otherwise have occurred. While this particular example does not convince me, I accept the feasibility of the process.
At the other extreme is what I call the freight train effect. Highballing
down the track, a freight train has enormous mass and momentum and,
short of switching tracks, cannot easily be diverted to another path. At
times the political, economic, social, and cultural worlds are like the
freight train. Any perturbations—or a minimal rewrite of history that
we introduce—will have fewer ramifications over time, bringing these
worlds back to the direction in which they were originally traveling. In
all likelihood the distribution of worlds along this continuum resembles a standard bell curve. Most worlds will cluster around the center,

and their number will diminish as we move out toward either end of the continuum.

My counterfactual probing of 1914 indicates that it is located somewhere between the mean and the butterfly end of the political-military continuum. Simple changes in personnel—most notably the survival of Franz Ferdinand—appear sufficient to have prevented war in August 1914 and to have moved the world further away from war in the years that followed. Franz Ferdinand would have become emperor in 1916, following the death by natural causes of the aging Franz Josef, and would almost certainly have introduced significant changes in the political structure of the empire. The resulting domestic conflict would have provided strong incentives to avoid foreign adventures, especially those that risked war. The simple act of saving Franz Ferdinand and Sophie from Princip's bullets would have led Austria-Hungary ever further away from the historical course it pursued in 1914. This is not the only plausible counterfactual that has this effect, so considering World War I must be considered highly contingent in its underlying and immediate causes.

If Europe had avoided war for three more years, Austrian, German, and Russian leaders in all likelihood would have become less risk prone. In Germany Moltke would have retired as chief of staff, and continued improvements in Russian railways and mobilization plans should have convinced his successor to reject his war plan in favor of a mobile defensive on both fronts. With a defensive strategy the need for preemption would have disappeared, and chancellor and kaiser alike would have been correspondingly more cautious in a crisis. Even when Erich von Falkenhayn, another general hell-bent on war, had succeeded Moltke as chief of staff, he would have found it much more difficult to convince political authorities to risk war when their security was not directly threatened. Had Austria not prodded Germany to declare war, neither the kaiser nor his chancellor would have taken the risk. And with Franz Ferdinand on the throne, Vienna would have been more inclined toward peace.

Making Russia more peaceful is more difficult because of the political weakness of the czarist regime. The country had largely recovered from the disastrous Russo-Japanese War of 1904–5 and the revolution that followed in its wake. The czar and his government nevertheless relied on a narrow, nationalist, and largely aristocratic elite for support. One reason that Russia sought to expand its influence in the Balkans and came to the support of Serbia in 1914 was to placate this constituency. The government was also under pressure to make the kinds of political concessions to the Duma that would have moved the political system toward a constitutional monarchy. Further to the left the government confronted a growing Socialist and revolutionary threat. Under almost any conditions, and especially adverse economic ones, the regime would have become weaker and more threatened. If the country was on the verge of revolution, or if Russian leaders feared a revolution if they went to war, they might have acted in a less aggressive way.

My analysis suggests that underlying political, strategic, and economic conditions in 1914 did not dictate war. The policies of Austria-Hungary, Germany, and Russia turned more on the choice of leaders, timing, and chance. With small changes in leadership or the timing of events, Europe could have weathered the crisis caused by the twin assassinations at Sarajevo just as it had earlier crises. For reasons I elaborated in Chapter 3, if war had been averted in 1914, it would have become increasingly less likely in 1917 and afterward.

SANDPILES AND MATTRESSES

Openness describes a system than cannot be isolated from other systems. The political, economic, and social worlds are open in the sense that they cannot be insulated from each other and are influenced by other kinds of developments as well. Outside developments routinely undermine general understandings of how politics or economics works.

Let me offer a telling example. In January 1999 Pope John Paul II made a scheduled stop in St. Louis during his tour of the United States; in St. Louis the pope pleaded with Governor Mel Carnahan of Missouri to commute to life imprisonment the sentence of a murderer scheduled for execution the next day. The governor honored the pope's request even though the condemned man's crime had been particularly heinous—a triple murder to which he had confessed—and he had no credible claim to leniency. The next person scheduled for execution in Missouri, Roy "Hog" Roberts, had attracted national attention because of the strong possibility that he was innocent, and numerous groups and prominent individuals, including the pope, appealed—without success—to Carnahan to commute Roberts's sentence. We can surmise that the governor, who had campaigned in support of the death penalty, was not about to commute the sentence of two murderers in a row, no matter how deserving the second offender might be. Had the pope gone to another state, arrived in St. Louis a few weeks later, and made his initial plea for the life of Roberts, the governor probably would have commuted his sentence. Studies of the death penalty and its application could not have predicted the outcome because they never would have considered the pope's itinerary a relevant variable.

Openness increases the likelihood of confluences: the coming together of independent chains of causation that produces an outcome none of these streams could have produced by themselves. I have characterized the social revolution of the 1960s and the origins of World War I this way. Elsewhere I have attributed the end of the Cold War to a confluence. Change in all realms is most often gradual, which is why most predictions are simply linear extensions of existing trends. They are often correct in the short term but never in the longer term because openness and confluences bring about evolution and phase transitions, rapid shifts from one state to another as when water freezes. At the turn of the nineteenth century editorials in the *New York Times* lamented the growth of horse-drawn traffic in Manhattan because of the health and other hazards it created. An official study examined the expected growth of horse traffic in the next fifty years and assumed that the demand would increase at the same rate. By extending this curve into the future they came to the disturbing conclusion that by 1950 the populated parts of Manhattan would be covered by as much as six feet of horse manure. They failed to consider the possibility that other means of transportation, notably, the automobile, would supplant the horse. And within a few years of this dire prediction, horses began to disappear from city streets.

Then there is the problem of what scientists call nonlinearity. We encounter it whenever events come together to produce an effect that is different from the result arrived at by simply adding together their expected consequences. One of the earliest descriptions of nonlinearity uses the example of the sandpile. We can drop grain after grain of sand to construct a roughly conical pile. At a certain point—always unpredictable—the addition of just one more grain topples the pile. Few political phenomena are quite as dramatic, although we might describe—metaphorically—the origins of the nuclear exchange in Chapter 5 this way. Crises were increasingly frequent; tensions mounted even when these crises were resolved; generals and political leaders in Britain and Germany came to see war as ever more likely; military forces remained on high alert and were more receptive to information indicating an attack. The grain of sand in this instance was the training tape fed into the active warning system. It triggered a catastrophe.

The confluence responsible for World War I was nonlinear in its effects on the risk-taking propensity of Austrian, German, and Russian leaders. So too was the military incident I invented to trigger the 1918–20 German constitutional crisis. I did not discuss it in detail but focused instead on its consequences and the conditions that led to them. The incident was triggered when military police arrested two teenage boys in Bremen for painting antimilitary graffiti on a barracks wall. The military police beat the boys up and held them incommunicado for several days while their parents, neighbors, and police searched for them. When they were finally released, one boy was rushed to a hospital and treated for internal bleeding. To make matters worse, the garrison commander and higher military authorities in Berlin defended the behavior of the soldiers and lieutenant responsible for mistreating the lads. The military's obstructionist tactics looked all the more outrageous in light of a local police inquiry that determined the boys were not politically motivated. They had painted their slogan on the wall—misspelling one word—as part of an initiation rite for a quasi-military club at their school.

What might have been a local affair quickly became a national one. Local demonstrations against the military, articles in the national press critical of the military, and demonstrations and further incidents elsewhere in Germany created a favorable environment in which Social Democratic and other reform-minded parliamentarians sought constitutional reform. Their cause was abetted by a widely publicized interview with a spokesman for the general staff who, having learned nothing from the Zabern affair, made insulting remarks about civilians.

Predicting how much of a sandpile will cave in when it collapses or in what direction this will occur is impossible. The same is true of political sand slides. Unlike the nuclear war in Chapter 5, the domestic crisis triggered by the military incident was open to diverse kinds of resolution. Had the government responded with a prompt public apology and court-martialed the officers involved, reaction to the incident would have been moderated and a more serious crisis averted. In this instance the sandpile would have remained largely intact—for the time being. Once the crisis escalated, the sandpile became ever more unstable, but the direction of its fall still could not be foreseen. Parliamentary victory, and with it the strengthening of constitutional democracy, and a military coup against the Parliament represent two different kinds of transformation of the prewar German political system. And they result in increasingly divergent worlds.

There is no reason to suppose that these are the only nonlinear interactions in my counterfactual worlds. Almost by definition most of them and their effects are unpredictable. Our counterfactual worlds accordingly remain as speculative as must any attempt to look far into the future. This uncertainty is troublesome only if we claim that one world, or something close to it, would have come to pass in the absence of World War I. This is not my intention. I posit these worlds only as representative of the classes of worlds that would have emerged in the absence of World War I. I use them to probe the envelope of possibilities of a world without this conflict.

WORSE WORLDS

Given the openness and nonlinearity of the social and political worlds, my best and worse worlds are only two of the many worlds that could have developed if the major European powers had avoided the catastrophe of World War I. We can speak with some degree of assurance only about the course of events in the immediate aftermath of our initial counterfactual.

In constructing counterfactual worlds we must distinguish between their onset and subsequent evolution. The initial counterfactual may be persuasive because what follows in the short term appears readily predictable. Without the twin assassinations at Sarajevo, Europe would have remained at peace at least through the end of 1914 and quite possibly for much longer. As we move further into the future from 1914, our crystal ball quickly clouds up. This is because counterfactuals set in motion all kinds of additional ones that can have entirely unforeseen consequences. Many developments would not have happened in the historical world, or they would have happened at a different time. Some of these will be wild cards—improbable events that seem unlikely or even imaginable in advance. Who, for example, would have predicted the Sarajevo assassinations, the runaway German inflation of the early 1920s, Chernobyl, the flight of Matthias Rust in his Cessna from Germany to Moscow's Red Square? Yet all these events had important political repercussions.

In my better world Emperor Franz Ferdinand ascends the Austrian throne in 1916 and introduces reforms that provoke a constitutional crisis that temporarily turns Austria-Hungary inward but ultimately sustains the longevity of the empire. In Germany the German Social Democratic Party (the Socialists) and the Zentrum Party (conservative to progressive Catholics) gain more seats in the Reichstag, primarily in response to the military's heavy-handed interference in civil affairs. The two parties, with the support of some liberals, have the votes to withhold funding from the army and navy, provoking a constitutional crisis.

In the German narrative the most important components are the SPD-Zentrum alliance, strong voter reaction against the army, some degree of division among the conservative opposition, and diplomatic initiatives by Britain and France that strengthen the opposition to the military and provide the context for follow-up efforts that achieve meaningful arms control. All these developments are eminently plausible, and their probabilities are related. If the army antagonizes the German public, which happens in my better world, the reform parties would benefit at the polls, the SPD and Zentrum would want to rein in the army, and liberals and Socialists in Britain and France might look for some way to strengthen their German counterparts. My narrative requires clever leadership of two German political parties and two great powers. Of equal importance, it assumes that the kaiser and his general staff recognize at some point during the constitutional crisis that they really have no choice but to reach an accommodation with the Reichstag. I develop this narrative because it paves the way for both my better and worse worlds. In the latter world the constitutional crisis ends differently than it did historically. The challenge to the kaiser and military by centrist and leftist parliamentarians provokes a coup, repression of Socialists and other democratically inclined groups and individuals, and consolidation of an even more authoritarian and repressive regime. In Austria-Hungary internal weakness makes the regime more dependent on Germany. Tensions remain high in both countries and between them and Britain and France.

This outcome of the German constitutional crisis is critical for the political development of the rest of Europe. In the better world democracy gradually becomes consolidated in Germany and to a lesser extent in Austria-Hungary. As Britain, France, the Low Countries, and Scandinavia are all constitutional democracies, and Germany is moving in this direction, the norm of democracy gradually becomes established and influences political developments elsewhere in Europe. Portugal and Spain benefit, and the trend toward democracy might have provided the impetus for the dysfunctional Italian parliamentary regime to reform itself, at least in part. As a result no Fascist dictatorship has a hold on Italy or the Iberian Peninsula. Russia undergoes a revolution, but the Bolshevik coup fails, and what ultimately emerges is an authoritarian regime that maintains the pretense of democratic forms. It is not unlike today's Russia in this respect.

In the version of the worst world that leads to nuclear war, the German coup consolidates military power, destroys the Socialist party, and strictly curtails the power of the Reichstag, trade unions, and press. A democratic underground develops; exiles conduct an active political life abroad and produce publications that are smuggled into their home countries. Austria-Hungary is more open than Germany or Russia, but the regime and police suppress as far as possible all expressions of nationalism directed against the empire. Southern Europe develops its own authoritarian regimes, as does post-Romanov Russia. Britain and France are robustly democratic but effectively isolated.

These differences have important implications for international relations. In the better world the spread of democracy, or at least parliamentary government, facilitates interstate cooperation on a wide range of issues, including arms control, and brings about a significant decline in tensions. By 1940 a great power war in Europe becomes all but unthinkable. Given this development, and the peaceful orientation of the United States, Japan is correspondingly more cautious in its foreign policy, and its military dictatorship is short lived. There are no arms races, no nuclear weapons, and no series of war-threatening crises.

In the worse world nuclear war gradually becomes more likely. By 1930 Europe is divided into two hostile camps; internal political differences reinforce external ones. By the 1940s modern weapons systems appear to give an advantage to the offensive, making everyone more insecure. By 1970 the situation is worse than it was in 1914 because the opposing alliances are more divided ideologically and the advantage of a nuclear first strike is seen as far more decisive than mobilization was in 1914. Once again Russia plays a destabilizing role but in a different way.

In the historical world internal weakness, and the belief that Russia would lose its status as a great power if it did not respond forcefully to any challenge, prompted its leaders to support Serbia in 1914. Russia's mobilization put it on a collision course with Austria and Germany. Because Russia was allied with France, mobilization in the east set in motion the Schlieffen Plan and with it the German invasion of Belgium and France. In the worse world in the 1960s and early 1970s Russia is outside each alliance system, and its adhesion to either would give it an important political and psychological advantage. Efforts by Heinz Kissinger to win Russia over to the German-Austrian camp trigger an acute crisis with Britain and France. Domestic and international problems reinforce each other as external conflicts justify domestic repression in Germany and Russia. Repression in turn exacerbates international tensions with France and Britain.

Authoritarian regimes and conflict in Europe in the worse world affect developments in Japan, making it more authoritarian and aggressive. Japan and the United States are at loggerheads. Increased tensions stimulate the arms race and lead to the development of nuclear weapons by all the great powers. Because Washington is focused on Asia, it does not play a major role in Europe, and Britain and France feel more threatened as a result.

Domestic and international developments had a profound impact on elite and popular culture in the twentieth century. In the better world the growth of democracy and expectation of peace provide a nurturing environment for European culture and science. Art, architecture, and the performing arts flourish and retain considerable national diversity, even though artistic movements and styles increasingly transcend national borders. In the absence of war European culture is more self-confident and, like European science, benefits from the contributions of people who otherwise died in World War I, the influenza pandemic, and at the hands of the Nazis or were forced to seek refuge on other continents. Europe retains its centrality in culture and science. Artists and scientists are respected and overwhelmingly democratic by orientation, so cultural developments reinforce political ones and help to move Europe further toward a peaceful world.

In the worst world, authoritarianism and repression are the order of the day and have a chilling effect on the arts. Many cultural figures and scientists leave their homelands for safer and more supportive environments, and those who remain behind must learn and practice self-censorship. Some consider themselves in internal exile. To a lesser extent this is true in the United States, where puritanical values remain ascendant, and censorship, both informal and legal, is widespread. The United States and Britain nevertheless gain from waves of artistic and scientific refugees, as well as those with other skills. As I have noted, ordinary people seeking to leave their homelands are much less welcome and find emigrating correspondingly more difficult.

By the 1970s my better and worse worlds have diverged markedly. These differences can be attributed to the different political paths of Austria and Germany in these two worlds. Key differences between these worlds—the degree of democracy, arms races and nuclear weapons, and international tensions—follow from this initial divergence. The political evolution of Austria and Germany represents a turning point because the developments that follow move them and the rest of Europe along increasingly divergent paths.

PEOPLE

Social scientists are fascinated by the so-called agency-structure problem. It refers to the relative importance of people versus context in determining behavior. If a fire breaks out in a theater, we can reasonably assume that every able-bodied person will rush to an exit. When people buy ice cream, in contrast, they choose their preferred flavor, although the distribution of these preferences may be predictable. At the microlevel individuals matter. Most theories in economics and political science— including those that attempt to explain war—assume the situations they describe more closely resemble fires in theaters than choices in ice cream parlors. Counterfactual probing of World War I indicates that, contrary to the expectation of these theories, agency was all important.

Franz Ferdinand's survival forestalls a Continental war in 1914 in the first instance because it deprives the war party in Vienna of the pretext it needs to go to war with Serbia. More important, Franz Ferdinand was convinced that Austria-Hungary's survival depended on peace with Russia and thus opposed any move in the Balkans that was likely to threaten good relations with Austria-Hungary's eastern neighbor. Although widely disliked by the Austrian political-military elite, the Thronfolger had enough authority to restrain Austrian foreign policy. Had he become emperor in 1916, his influence would have grown considerably. Franz Ferdinand is also critical to the subsequent world because he introduces reforms that significantly alter the political future of Austria-Hungary. This scenario cannot be dismissed as speculation because, as I noted in Chapter 3, Franz Ferdinand's correspondence and notebooks give ample indications of the kinds of policies he intended to pursue as emperor.

In Germany the kaiser, Bethmann-Hollweg, and Moltke guided policy in the July 1914 crisis. Their support of Austria made possible its ultimatum to Serbia that led to a Continental war. All three German leaders were critical in different ways. Moltke hated France and desperately wanted to humiliate it by means of war. He rigged war games to show that an offensive was possible and that a defensive was not, misled chancellor and kaiser alike about the military situation, and went behind their backs to urge action on his Austrian counterparts. Bethmann-Hollweg was peacefully inclined but lacked the courage of his convictions. He was misled by Moltke and too subservient to Wilhelm. The kaiser in turn was insecure, mercurial, and full of bluster but weak and susceptible to petty individual and national jealousies. He looked down on France, had a love-hate relationship with England, greatly overrated his own cleverness, and valued his commitment to support his fellow monarch Franz Josef more than he did the national interest of his own country. In my worse world scenario Wilhelm reluctantly goes along with his generals' demand for a coup against the Socialists.

Would different leaders have acted more or less responsibly? Unlike Franz Ferdinand, whom we can bring back from the grave, we are stuck with the kaiser, who lived until 1941. Nor is there any readily available pretext for removing Bethmann-Hollweg and Moltke. Former chancellor Bernhard von Bülow—in office from 1900 to 1909—insists that he would have exercised restraint in 1914. But his claim was made in his postwar memoirs so must be treated with caution, and arranging for him to stay in office requires more than a simple minimal rewrite of history. These were the leaders at the time of our imagined military coup in 1919. The kaiser was still on the throne. Moltke would have retired, but his successor would likely have shared his views. Bethmann-Hollweg stepped down in March 1917 after unsuccessfully opposing undeclared submarine warfare in the Atlantic and might well have retired before 1919 in the absence of a war. Without much fuss we can appoint a successor who is either a pliant nonentity or a man of skill and courage who might have restrained the kaiser and stood up to the generals.

World War I was highly contingent if only because of the critical difference the survival of Franz Ferdinand would have made for Austrian policy. Vienna would neither have sought a blank check from Berlin nor invaded Serbia. Russia would not therefore have mobilized, triggering a German invasion of France and a continental war. Austria-Hungary would have developed differently with Franz Ferdinand as emperor. The German turning point of 1919 is more problematic because the inclinations of the kaiser and his general staff would have been more in the direction of confrontation than conciliation when confronted with assertive parliamentarians. It is easier to make the case for a coup than a parliamentary victory and constitutional monarchy. This outcome, the foundation of the better world, requires more careful staging. The military must do something outrageous along the lines of the Zabern affair and become intransigent in the face of criticism. An election must be held in which the Social Democrats and Zentrum increase their parliamentary representation, a trend already in place. It is reasonable to assume that they would win more votes still, some cast in protest against the military, in an election that followed renewed civil-military confrontation. It is also possible that the chancellor, although appointed by the kaiser, would nevertheless understand that his country's national interest required a political settlement along the lines I describe. Finally conciliatory overtures from Britain and France would make such an accommodation more likely. As is so often the case, neither agency nor structure is determining. What counts is their interplay.

People are critical at numerous other junctures in the historical and counterfactual worlds. Without Hitler, conjuring a right-wing or military dictatorship and a war of revenge in the east against Poland is easy, but not a Holocaust. Some president other than Franklin Roosevelt might have been less committed to engaging the US Navy in the Atlantic against the German submarine threat while the United States was technically at peace. Another president might also have been less imaginative and politically skilled and not have conceived or secured congressional authorization for the Lend-Lease Program. Both moves were critical to Britain's survival and Hitler's decision to declare war on the United States in the immediate aftermath of Pearl Harbor. Had Hitler not done so, the United States would have fought a war in the Pacific against Japan, and World War II in Europe would have developed differently.

In our worst world the difference between a tense peace and limited nuclear war is a crisis in the 1970s. A training tape somehow gets into the live nuclear warning system and triggers it. This may sound farfetched, but something similar happened in the real world. In 1980, in response to a computer chip malfunction, B–52 bombers were readied for take-off, and the airborne command post of the Pacific commander was launched. If the error had not been diagnosed in a timely way, almost a hundred B-52s would have been sent toward their fail-safe position, and messages would have been sent to alert ICBM crews in missile silos and to conventional forces in Europe and Korea. President Reagan would have been awakened at approximately 2:30 a.m. and told that he had minutes to evacuate Washington, decide on the country's war plan, and order a nuclear response. We do not know how Reagan would have responded, but in our imaginary world the British prime minister fails to exercise adequate restraint, with catastrophic results. His German counterpart was also overly receptive to military pleas for retaliation.

In 1948 Hans J. Morgenthau, the leading realist theorist of his time, decried the Cold War because it had reduced international relations "to the primitive spectacle of two giants eyeing each other with watchful suspicion." He considered emerging bipolarity conducive to peace but agency even more important. Crises between the superpowers were inevitable, and peace would turn on the moral qualities of statesmen. Had he written about international politics in our worse world, he would almost certainly have made the same observation. In the historical world President Kennedy and Soviet General Secretary Khrushchev displayed courage and insight at the height of the Cuban Missile Crisis when they took security and political risks for the sake of peace. In 1914 and the war variant of our worse scenario, leaders did not rise to the occasion. In the more peaceful narrative crises are resolved, but the future is threatening and unclear.

THINKING ABOUT OUR WORLD

What do our counterfactual worlds teach us about World War I and its consequences? My answer comes in two parts: substantive and conceptual.

The most important conceptual lesson is the contingency of events. World War I was highly contingent in its underlying and immediate causes. Had the confluence I described not occurred, or if the assassinations at Sarajevo had been prevented, there would have been no World War I in 1914. For reasons I provided, war became increasingly unlikely after 1917. So there was something like a three-year window when war could have been triggered. It would have required another acute crisis and equally irresponsible behavior by the great powers. The only country with any interest in starting a war was Austria-Hungary and then only a limited one against Serbia. With Franz Ferdinand in the driver's seat—not the backseat of his touring car—this would not have happened.

I have made the case that this contingency is equally evident in the subsequent evolution of European political systems. Germany, Austria-Hungary, Italy, and Russia were all politically unstable, and I have examined various permutations of political development in all four countries. I looked at the two extremes: a world in which all four evolve in the same way—toward more democratic or authoritarian regimes— and one in which the reverse is true. Internal developments in all these countries are highly contingent, as I tried to demonstrate in the German case. The coevolution is also contingent but significantly linked. We can expect that if Germany and Austria become more authoritarian, or more democratic, this development will have a major impact on the political development of neighboring countries. At a certain point the spread of either authoritarianism or democracy will become more difficult to resist elsewhere in Europe. This is demonstrably the case with democracy in Europe after 1945. It does not mean that every Continental government would have become democratic, but a general movement to this effect certainly would have occurred.

The second general lesson concerns the close connections across social domains. I have illustrated some of these connections in the biographies of real and imagined people. Their lives develop differently, sometimes radically so, across the better and worse worlds. World War I offers a graphic demonstration of the way in which politics influences culture. As a result of the war many Europeans lost faith in themselves and their culture. This pessimism had a profound effect in the arts, where it cut short the kind of experimentation that had characterized the prewar decade. It affected philosophy, where the dominant theme became the need for order, reflected in such diverse projects as analytical philosophy and the Vienna school's attempt to provide logical warrants for scientific claims. In architecture the severe, angular Bauhaus style challenged the earlier emphasis on decoration and individuality. Modern design and architecture not only reflect contemporary values but also help to shape them. People who grow up and work in an urban environment of narrow streets, intimate squares, individualized storefronts, and heavily frequented cafes think differently about themselves and their social relationships than people accustomed to driving rather than walking and working in large, tall buildings in cities with few public spaces but many suburban malls.

Close and poorly understood relationships exist across all these seemingly discrete domains. We might think of the social world as something akin to a spring mattress, where pressure at any point, against only a few springs, is transmitted throughout the mattress. In some directions the pressure might be alleviated as the springs adjust to the new forces and in other directions amplified as it intensifies existing ones. These relationships are nonlinear and almost impossible to predict, although the new feel of the mattress is quite evident. These relationships work in the long and short term and often have consequences diametrically opposed to those envisaged by relevant actors. Linear perspective and printing are examples of the latter. Deeply religious artists and printers who sought more effective ways of bringing people closer to god introduced these innovations. Artists and printers benefited from patrons with similar aims. In the long term both innovations facilitated the emergence of the autonomous individual and a more secular world.

For all these reasons prediction is difficult in the short term and all but impossible in the long term. The ancient Greeks were among the first to recognize the problem of unintended consequences. In Sophocles's *Oedipus* the eponymous hero tries to escape the prophecy that he will kill his father and bed his mother. His actions serve only to bring about the fate he so desperately wants to avoid. Human behavior is almost always goal directed, but we never act in a vacuum. What other people do influences the outcome of our actions, which is the product of a complex and often nonlinear process of aggregation. This phenomenon should make us cautious about our immediate and long-range expectations.

Humans have a propensity to believe that big events have big causes, but no evidence exists to support this folk wisdom. As my sandpile example illustrates, minor events can also have large consequences. This was true of World War I, where Princip's bullets set in motion an unintended chain of events, as did the terrorist attacks of 9/11 and July 2005 in London. In Chapter 2, I offered the additional example of Elian. Had he drowned, Al Gore would have won Florida and, with it, the presidential election. As a consequence the United States would not have invaded Iraq. Many other minor events in my counterfactual worlds have the potential, like the Sarajevo assassinations and the German constitutional crisis, to put these worlds on very different trajectories.

The most likely world, in my judgment, is one close to what I imagine to be the mean of all the possible worlds in which World War I does not occur. In this world neither Germany nor Austria would undergo the dramatic domestic transformations both did between 1916 and 1921 in my better counterfactual world. The Continent would have mixed democratic and authoritarian regimes, tensions among European states would have diminished at a slower rate, the pace of economic and scientific development would have been less than it was in the better world but faster than in the worse world. Neither atomic nor thermonuclear weapons would exist.

Germany's political development is the principal determining feature of these several worlds. In the most likely world a constitutional crisis probably occurs, sometime between 1914 and 1920, but not a major transformation of the political system, with the Reichstag facing down the emperor and the military, or through a coup. The German political system evolves more gradually. In 1914 it was a mixed system, which was one source of its tensions. Germany had a relatively free press, a quasi-independent bureaucracy and legal system, and a freely elected parliament in which the Socialists had become the largest party. Foreign and military affairs were nevertheless the reserve of the kaiser and the officials he appointed to advise him. The chancellor and ministers were also responsible to the kaiser, not to the Reichstag. Suffrage, especially in Prussia, was far from universal, and electoral districts favored rural conservative parts of the country. We can imagine change taking place in fits and starts but with the overall effect of increasing the authority of the Reichstag and civil authorities in general vis-à-vis the army and leading to significant electoral reform. This in turn would have strengthened democratic and progressive forces. Such a transition could only have been helped by several decades of peace and a declining perception of foreign threats.

This perceptual change could have occurred in several ways. Even in the absence of a long costly war, another revolution in Russia was a real possibility. Internal unrest in Russia, and even more its implosion, would have reduced the military threat to Germany in the east. Following a German switch to a defensive strategy on the western front, the generals would have found it increasingly difficult to make the case that France posed any offensive threat. Add to this the possibility of arms control in the form of a naval agreement with Britain and perhaps a mutual agreement with France to call fewer young men to the colors every year. A naval agreement was in the mutual interest of Britain and Germany, given the escalating costs of dreadnoughts and their consumption of steel that could otherwise be used for productive purposes. By 1925 the military competition between Germany and its Anglo-French antagonists might have come to resemble the Cold War of the 1970s, when the superpowers embraced arms control to limit the risk of war. Perceptive leaders and analysts in the United States and the Soviet Union recognized that the arms race, once an expression of East-West tensions, had become one of the principal causes of those tensions.

Another development promoting German security would have been its continuing economic penetration of eastern Europe and Russia. In 1914 leading German industrialists, bankers, and shipping magnates told the kaiser that peace was in Germany's interest. A week before Sarajevo, the Hamburg banker Max Warburg advised the kaiser against war. "Germany," Warburg insisted, "becomes stronger with every year of peace." By this he meant that investment, trade, and cultural influence—what today would be called soft power—would soon make

Germany the undisputed master of the Continent. By 1925 German investment in Russia might have been on a par with that of France, or perhaps have exceeded it, making St. Petersburg correspondingly more cautious in its foreign policy.

As the German language and culture increasingly penetrated the East, someone in Germany might have conceptualized soft power or something like it. Soft power would have been an appealing alternative to the dominant military-based discourse of geopolitics. Within Germany affluence and the material values it fosters would have become more pronounced, as they do everywhere in response to economic development. The Pacific Rim, and especially China, provides graphic contemporary evidence of this phenomenon. Young people intent on making careers and money—that is, most German youth by 1930—would have considered military service a nuisance, if not an unnecessary atavism prolonged only to sustain the military establishment. The general staff, with its antiquated Prussian values and hostility to modernity—military technology aside—would have become a principal subject of mockery in cabarets and popular media. Legal action against such caricatures and their perpetrators would have intensified antimilitary sentiment. With diminishing public support the power of the military would have waned, and that of reform-minded parties and politicians would have increased correspondingly. Barring an acute crisis or a coup, the gradual transition to parliamentary democracy would have gathered enough momentum to become all but inevitable. As for a coup, if it came late enough in the game—say, in the late 1920s or early 1930s—it would have aroused the immediate opposition of the parliament and most of the German public. The appropriate analogy here is to the attempted coup against Mikhail Gorbachev in August 1991. It failed miserably in the face of unexpected local opposition and even stronger opposition in the non-Russian republics. The coup's collapse hastened the end of communism and the Soviet Union.

In this most likely world scenario, or its many variants, we move more gradually toward my better world. Dangers remain, but they are of a different kind. German domination of eastern Europe, achieved by peaceful economic means, hastens the region's development. This could mute or intensify nationality conflicts depending on how evenly the wealth is spread and how German and local authorities respond to minorities. In a worst-case scenario, we can imagine a Polish rebellion in the aftermath of a Russian revolution and the proclamation of a Polish state that lays claim to much of German Pomerania and East Prussia, lands inhabited by Poles. German suppression of Polish independence and military occupation of Polish lands could provoke an Iraq-like insurgency and a long, costly, and inconclusive struggle between rebels and occupying forces. German youth and the Socialists might protest against this war of occupation, prompting a more serious domestic crisis reminiscent of the United States during the Vietnam War. Such a conflict could hasten the transformation of Germany, for better or worse.

In 1914 Germany was the richest, most educated, and most technologically developed country in Europe. Russia aside, it was also the most populous. Imagining a democratic, peaceful Europe in the absence of a democratic, self-confident, and physically secure Germany is impossible. In a more fundamental sense Germany was the critical test case for the transition from the medieval to modern worlds. In *A Cultural Theory of International Relations,* I argue that the most fundamental cause of war in 1914 was the intellectual and economic changes associated with modernity. The emergence of the concept of the autonomous individual and the economic development it fostered gave rise to the bourgeoisie, a new class with new values. Throughout continental Europe aristocrats, the primary beneficiaries of the old order, felt threatened. For reasons I make clear in this chapter, this feeling of threat was most intense in Germany.

By 1914 three gradients characterized Europe, shaping, if not determining, the foreign policy orientations of national elites. The first gradient, which ran from west to east, tracked the size of the middle class. It was largest in Britain; smaller in France, Germany, and Austria-Hungary; and smallest in Russia. The industrial revolution had begun in Britain, and even before the late eighteenth century, the British Isles had a large middle class because of the high level of commercial activities.

The second gradient also ran from west to east. It was the extent to which aristocrats were disposed to reach political and social accommodations with the rising middle class. This willingness was greatest in Britain, where aristocrats had long made commercial investments and married wealthy nonaristocrats. The various reform acts of Parliament during the nineteenth and early twentieth centuries extended the franchise and began to impose fairer forms of taxation. In France the revolution brought about radical changes, only partially reversed by the post-Napoleonic restoration. In the Third Republic, founded in 1871, the middle class became the dominant political, economic, and social force in the country. This was not the case farther east. In Germany the bourgeoisie had made great strides. However, much more than in England, the middle class imitated the values and practices of aristocrats. This did not make the middle class any more acceptable; if anything, the reverse was true.

The third gradient had to do with the extent to which control of foreign and military policy remained in aristocratic hands. Here the gradient ran from east to west. In Russia, Austria-Hungary, and Germany foreign and military policy was the preserve of the monarch and his aristocratic advisers. In France and Britain foreign and military policy was a matter of national concern, with participation by diverse constituencies. On the Continent, with the exception of France, officers and diplomats were aristocrats. They advocated policies that advanced or defended their honor and that of their state. Many increasingly came to regard war as beneficial, even necessary, to preserve the old order and, with it, their privileges and those of their class. German, Austro-Hungarian, and Russian leaders were accordingly more risk prone than their Anglo-French counterparts. This only increased in 1914 because of the confluence I described.

Germany was the decisive country in regard to war and peace. Austria-Hungary could not—and would not—provoke a war without German support. Russia in turn was weak enough not to harbor aggressive military aims but ready to draw the sword if its leaders perceived their honor and status as a great power to be at risk. World War I in the most fundamental sense was the result of the material and ideational changes associated with modernity. However, that does not make it inevitable. As the better and worse worlds indicate, in another few years Europe, and Germany in particular, would have evolved in ways that would make such a war less likely. The tragedy of 1914 is that an appropriate catalyst for war appeared in a narrow three-year window when Austrian, German, and Russian leaders were irresponsible and risk prone.

THE REST OF THE WORLD

My analysis has concentrated on Europe and North America, although I have said a few words in passing about India and Japan. India was the largest and most important nonsettler colony in the British Empire. Historically and counterfactually Japan was the major power in Asia for most of the twentieth century. China was a populous backwater, largely at the mercy of the great powers.

Latin America has been another peripheral player in the world's economy, politics, and, until quite recently, cultural life. From the US perspective, Latin America has been a source of cheap raw materials, immigrants, and drugs. Since the turn of the century Brazil has become a major economic power, and its soccer and music have worldwide appeal. Its trajectory does not change much in any of our counterfactual worlds. In the better world Central America avoids considerable bloodshed because the United States does not support right-wing regimes, as it did in the historical world out of fear of the spread of communism. Colombia and Mexico are more stable and less violent because the demand for illegal drugs in the United States is less. In the worse world the United States is not as rich, so the demand for goods is less and fewer Latin immigrants are going north. In both worlds Washington considers the region its private reserve and continues to act as kingmaker, often in crude ways. As in the historical world Latin American has much respect for US power but no love of Yankee domination.

Africa and the Middle East are the most turbulent regions. In Africa the culprits are obvious: colonialism and postcolonial kleptocracies. The imposition of colonial empire everywhere south of the Sahara resulted in political units with arbitrarily drawn borders that ignored tribal, cultural, and linguistic groupings. The British pursued a kind of divide-and-rule policy that pitted one tribal group against another. Although the French and British built infrastructure, especially schools to disseminate their languages, and brought some talented students to the metropole to continue their studies, colonialism existed for the benefit of the colonizer. Benefits to the colonized were merely incidental or the result of efforts of religious and other charitable organizations.

Countries in Africa and the Middle East for the most part achieved independence in the 1960s, and what followed was often worse. Ethnic conflict, civil war, and the breakdown of order or government by corrupt politicians more interested in foreign bank accounts than the interests of their people consumed country after country. The former colonial powers and the United States were generally complicit with these regimes as they made sweetheart deals of every kind with them. In return the former colonial powers and the United States often provided these regimes military hardware necessary to retain power.

African leaders and intellectuals blame colonialism for their country's backwardness, as do many of their Middle Eastern counterparts. This argument is patently self-serving, designed to buttress self-esteem and deflect criticism at home and abroad. There can be no doubt about the failures of colonialism. However, indigenous elites bear their share of guilt for the pitiful conditions of many of their countries, and the elites' share increases at every decade of remove from colonialism. The HIV pandemic is another curse of the underdeveloped world, more deadly for Africans than the influenza epidemic was for Asians and Europeans in 1918–19. Conspiracy theories to the contrary, it is an act of nature but one made much worse by existing social practices and the long-standing resistance of many governments to acknowledge or confront the problem.

The Middle East is better off than Africa but still in the thrall of authoritarian regimes. It remains to be seen whether the so-called Arab Spring will bring about meaningful change in this regard. For almost seventy years Arab intellectuals have blamed their region's economic and political backwardness and turmoil on Western imperialism. Once again, this rhetorical device and psychological defense is effective against acknowledging indigenous causes.

As in the case of nineteenth- and early twentieth-century Europe, modernization has exacerbated many problems of the non-Western world. The absence of colonialism would not have made much difference. Israel is the other Middle Eastern whipping boy, and here too much of the rhetoric is patently self-serving. In both the better and worse worlds, Israel does not exist because there has been no Hitler, no World War II, and no Holocaust. There is still a Yishuv, as the Jewish settlement in Palestine was known, and tensions between Jewish settlers and local Arabs still bedevil everyone because they lay claim to the same land. In the better world, these tensions were muted, and suppressed when necessary, by the international consortium that had established a protectorate in the Holy Land. In the worse world the Ottoman Empire lasts longer, and when it collapses, the major European powers struggle to establish spheres of influence. Here too the European presence moderates conflict while spurring the development of indigenous nationalism.

In both counterfactual worlds fewer Jews live in Palestine as they have had less incentive to leave Europe and other parts of the Middle East. In the worse world this incentive still exists but is restricted to eastern Europe and Russia, where nationality conflict and revolution bring about pogroms. Wealthier western Jews help poorer eastern Jews emigrate, as they did in the historical world. In both counterfactual worlds, the United States is more closed to immigration so more Jews go to western Europe and Palestine. The population of Palestine grows, and Germany, Britain, and France compete for influence in the region and hold themselves out as protectors of the Jews. These countries are also interested in access to oilfields located in Iraq, the Persian Gulf, and Persia but see no contradiction in their pursuit of oil and support of the Jews. This is because nationalism in the Middle East remains a local phenomenon—as it was historically until after World War II and the partition of Palestine—and Palestinian-Jewish tensions have not become linked to larger regional issues, let alone to a Cold War.

I have already discussed India. In better and worse worlds it achieves dominion status in lieu of independence although for diametrically opposed reasons. Autonomy comes early enough to satisfy most Indians, and economic development is more rapid in the absence of multiple Indian-Pakistani wars and the large military establishments both sides maintain. In historical India the defense establishment is bloated because of the 1962 war with China and the cold war with it that followed. In both counterfactual worlds China is neither a rising power nor in possession of a nuclear arsenal, so Indians feel no need to develop nuclear weapons. Hindus and Muslims still clash, but religious conflict is muted in comparison with the historical world. India is of course a much larger state as it includes what are now Pakistan and Bangladesh. All along its peripheries India confronts problems with dissident ethnic groups and conflicts between them and lowland neighbors. Some periodically erupt into violence.

China has been a rising power ever since the mainland was reunified and the People's Republic was proclaimed in 1949. Many now expect it to become the dominant economic power in the next few decades. Both counterfactual worlds forestall this trajectory, as colonialism lasts longer and the Japanese do not invade China in the 1930s.

China's history is quite different in both counterfactual worlds. Without the Soviet Union China's Communists would have been much less powerful. Without the Japanese invasion Mao's Red Army would not have been able to mobilize support on the basis of its resistance to the foreign invader. In all probability the conflict for power in China would have been between competing warlords, with the Communists playing a bit part. That any one faction would have emerged victorious is unlikely. Certainly keeping this from happening was in the interests of the great powers. Germany, Britain, France, Russia, Japan, and the United States might have supported opposing warlords in return for economic privileges. This scenario is equally likely in the better and worse worlds. Thus the trajectory of China is very different in either counterfactual world from what it is in the historical world.

Almost from the beginning of recorded history Chinese civilization compared favorably with any other along any dimension worth discussing. From the time of its unification in 221 BCE, at the end of the Qin wars, China was at least the military and economic equal of the Roman Empire and in many ways more advanced. China was always the world's most populous country, and up to the end of the eighteenth century its population was also among the healthiest. It consumed more calories, benefited from better public health, and was on average better off and longer lived than its Indian, Middle Eastern, and European counterparts.

China's science and technology were unrivaled. Consider, for example, oceanic exploration, which draws on diverse forms of technology. Chinese envoys had been sailing into the Indian Ocean since the late second century BCE. In 674 private explorers like Daxi Hongtong reached the southern tip of the Arabian Peninsula. In 1401 China's Yongle emperor seized the throne and ruled for twenty-two years. Between 1405 and 1433 he sent seven flag-waving expeditions into the Indian Ocean under Admiral Zheng He. The first expedition was composed of 62 sea-going junks, 225 support vessels, and 27,780 men. It traded in silk and ceramics and refused to sell weapons on the grounds that the expeditions were messengers of peace and it was wrong "to bully weaker peoples." Chinese expeditions went as far afield as Madagascar, off the coast of southern Africa.

Chinese junks weighed more than 3,000 tons, which made them ten times the size of the largest European ships of the time. They measured 164 × 32 feet, compared to the 30-foot length of the *Santa Maria,* Columbus's flagship on his voyage to the Caribbean. The Chinese hulls were made plank by plank and fitted together with wooden dowels, which made them less fragile and more watertight than their European counterparts. They had separate bulkheads, unlike European ships. Chinese junks had nine masts with bamboo, rather than canvas, sails, which opened and closed like Venetian blinds. The construction and steering of the junks meant they could sail closer to the wind, and they also benefited from advanced navigational instruments. The few military encounters between European vessels and Asian ships that fitted with Chinese technology (i.e., Javanese and Indian craft) proved the latter's superiority.

Europe pulled ahead in the late eighteenth century in science, technology, military capability, and economic development and by the late nineteenth century in public health and life expectancy. These gaps increased markedly in the twentieth century, and China began to close them only in the last decades of that century. From a long-term historical perspective China's closing in on, and perhaps surpassing, the West would return history to the path it had been on for almost two thousand years. Viewed this way, one could regard the rise of China as inevitable and Western hegemony a short-lived deviation—a mere two centuries—from the norm. Alternatively we can reject the past as any determinant of the future, and indeed I have made strong arguments against linear projections. What insight can our counterfactual analysis offer into the question of China's future?

In an earlier collaborative study of the phenomenal rise of the West in the modern era, my colleagues and I argued that it had many causes, most of them contingent. The same can be said about China's cultural, military, and scientific superiority for almost two millennia. Above all it depended on the creation and maintenance of central authority over a vast land area and population. Nothing was inevitable about this development, and in its absence the landmass we call China would have developed into different political units with different languages. In contrast the absence of unification and the division of what we call Europe into numerous competing political units accounts for Western superiority, at least in part. Competition provided strong incentives for effective state building and the improvement of military technology and tactics. The West also had structural advantages in the modern era, especially the colocation of iron, coal, and river transport to bring the raw materials, or finished goods, to urban markets. In China, in contrast, iron and coal were located in the northern and southern extremities, and the rivers ran west to east. The country accordingly developed a different kind of economy based on new settlements and local production.

For these reasons imagining that the industrial revolution might have begun in China or the Honshu Plain in Japan is almost impossible. So the West had a key advantage in the modern era, but its economic, military, and cultural success ultimately depended on more arbitrary human factors. If we substitute China for Europe and look forward rather than backward, this mix looks the same and is nicely illustrated by comparing my counterfactual worlds with the historical one.

In the better and worse worlds China's weakness and internal division continue beyond 1949 and perhaps into the next century. This is attributable to the prolongation of colonialism and the failure of the

Bolshevik coup in Russia. The Guomindang, or its equivalent, tries to unify China but cannot overcome the power of local warlords, especially because many receive support from the colonial powers. The Western powers, Russia, and Japan see keeping China weak and divided as in their interest. The Communists also remain weak and, without the Soviet Union, weaker still.

In the nuclear war variant of the worst world, China may have a better chance at unification and development. The European powers are temporarily crippled, and it is not inconceivable that the United States would support unification as a means of checking the ambitions of Japan and Russia. If the Chinese government extends its authority to the north, and especially to Manchuria, the most industrialized province, it might have a chance at more rapid economic development.

There are important comparisons and trade-offs with the historical world to consider. China benefited in the historical world, at least in the short term, from an authoritarian regime that was committed to unification and development. It was willing and able to use force, often on a massive scale, to achieve these ends. Imagining Chinese unification and development in the absence of force is difficult. The transformation of China nevertheless involved enormous human costs, especially in the era of Mao Zedong. The Great Leap Forward (1958–61) was an ill-fated attempt to industrialize the country as rapidly as possible. Estimates of the number of people killed in the process range from 18 to 45 million. The Cultural Revolution (1966–76), also the brainchild of Mao, may have killed a million more. Estimates of the number of people killed by the Chinese Communists under Mao Zedong run as high as 40 million. The Great Leap Forward and Cultural Revolution set development back by more than a decade. The current regime has been more responsible in every way but is demonstrably corrupt, authoritarian, and stifling to individual and group creativity. It has the potential to become a serious impediment to the growth of China.

In our two counterfactual worlds, no government is Communist, and the economies of China's quasi-independent units are tied more closely to the economies of Japan and the West. In the short run this would have been disadvantageous to China, as it would have made it a supplier of cheap raw materials and labor and a receiver of expensive manufactured goods. In the longer term it might have proved beneficial but only if a less authoritarian regime unified and governed the country. Imagining how a democratic regime could have succeeded in doing this is difficult. So really the best one can hope for is an authoritarian regime that gradually evolves into a more democratic one. This of course remains a possibility in the historical world, and, if it comes to pass, it will prompt the conclusion that the historical world, despite its horrendous costs, was close to the best world one can reasonably imagine for twentieth-century China.

Counterfactual examination suggests that World War I brought us neither the best nor worst of worlds. Our world is something in between but closer to the worse one. The major difference between the historical and worst worlds is that a European war came earlier rather than later. Destructive as it was, it did not involve the use of nuclear weapons. It was, however, inconclusive in that it paved the way for a second, even more destructive, world war with major theaters of operations outside Europe. Although the war was fought primarily with conventional weapons, two atomic bombs were dropped on Japan. They were probably unnecessary to compel a Japanese surrender, but this was not evident to the White House at the time. In the worst world a European war is postponed in the first half of the twentieth century, but acute tensions remain. They encourage the development of more lethal weapons and prompt a cold war similar to the one between the superpowers. Nuclear weapons and their delivery systems, initially an expression of the conflict, quickly become one of its principal causes. In the nuclear counterfactual Britain and Germany exchange nuclear bombs, and Germany also destroys targets elsewhere in western Europe. The resulting fatalities are considerably less than those for either world war, but the training tape incident could easily have led to an all-out nuclear war whose casualties would have been much greater.

The worst world differs from the historical world in other important ways. The fictional world has no Hitler, no Nazis, and no Holocaust, although anti-Semitism is rife and remains so for a long time. The postwar European success story required the decisive defeat and occupation of Germany, the extirpation of the Nazi regime, and a continuing US political, economic, and military presence in western Europe. Defeat of Germany also meant that eastern Europe would remain under the Soviet control for almost fifty years. None of this happens in the variant of the worst world that has a nuclear exchange, although the prospect of a nuclear annihilation remains real.

As I noted, I think some version of the first counterfactual world is the most likely scenario in the absence of World War I. If so, Europe would not have gone down the path to World War II and would have avoided the catastrophes of the 1930s and 1940s. To equal these horrors in Europe, we must go back to the Thirty Years' War of the seventeenth century or Great Plague of the fourteenth. Any version of the second counterfactual world is vastly preferable because a world without World War I, World War II, or anything like it is extremely difficult to imagine. The second counterfactual world is also better in the sense that it is more pluralistic: it has no superpowers, English is not the lingua franca, Europe retains its central role in political and cultural affairs, and more indigenous cultures remain vibrant.

The United States is both more and less parochial. It is more inward looking in the sense of receiving fewer immigrants from Europe, especially those from the economic, scientific, and cultural elites. Its indigenous culture is more restrictive because Victorian values survive longer than they did in the historical world. But it is also less parochial in that Americans interested in art, science, and medicine are more likely to study in Europe, learn its languages, and return home more cosmopolitan. Europe receives a constant trickle of Americans for that reason, but in the twentieth century, the line of American expats would have become a stream and then a fast-flowing river, as it was about to in 1914.

Historical America is undoubtedly a better place than either the better or worst world. It fought in both world wars but suffered the fewest casualties of any of the major combatants. It and Canada were the only ones whose homelands were not subjected to repeated aerial bombardment. The United States gained economically and politically from both wars and achieved something close to hegemony in the immediate postwar era. It also benefited from an influx of talented refugees. The world wars unintentionally fostered greater tolerance among Americans, making them more receptive to granting civil rights and equality to religious and ethnic minorities, African Americans, women, and homosexuals.

None of these outcomes could have been predicted in advance, and some are downright counterintuitive. Who would have imagined, for example, that even before the United States entered either world war, industry would gear up to supply overseas combatants and attract large numbers of southern blacks as workers? Or that the children of these migrants would receive better educations and professional opportunities and would spearhead a successful civil rights movement? Another example of unintended consequences is the development of computing to solve military problems. Within two generations its spin-offs were responsible for the information revolution, a transformation in every way as profound as the industrial revolution. Nor would anyone have taken seriously in 1945 the prediction that France and Germany would quickly become reconciled and, together with Italy and the Benelux countries, lay the foundation for a peaceful, prosperous Europe with many open borders, a widely shared currency, and a plethora of supra-national institutions.

This investigation of the past should teach us to be wary about predictions. They are generally linear and fail to take into account system-level effects, confluences, or events that bring about major transformations. Linear projections rest on the assumption that the future will be more or less like the present *and* that we know why the present is the way it is. Our understanding of the present is based on our understanding of the past, and that, I have shown, rests on the belief that past events were overdetermined. After all, nobody would draw universal lessons from events they recognize to be highly contingent. The more we use counterfactuals to unpack history and reveal its contingency, the more we see the fallacy in drawing lessons from these events. Many of our assumptions and theories about international relations come from the putative lessons of World Wars I and II. These lessons rest on the untested—and generally unsupportable—assumption that these events are general, not unique, overdetermined, and not highly contingent. Caveat emptor!

Suggested Reading

CHAPTER 1

The classic work on cognitive biases and heuristics is Daniel Kahneman, Paul Slovic, and Amos Tversky, *Judgment Under Uncertainty: Heuristics and Biases* (New York: Cambridge University Press, 1982). For psychological research on counterfactuals and the conditions in which people invent them, see Neal J. Roese, "The Functional Basis of Counterfactual Thinking," *Journal of Personality and Social Psychology* 66 (1994): 805–18; Neal J. Roese and James M. Olson, eds., *What Might Have Been: The Social Psychology of Counterfactual Thinking* (Mahwah, NJ: Erlbaum, 1995); David R. Mandel, "Counterfactuals, Emotions and Context," *Cognition and Emotion* 17 (2003): 139–59; Matthew N. McMullen, "Affective Contrast and Assimilation in Counterfactual Thinking," *Journal of Experimental Social Psychology* 65 (1999): 812–21; L. J. Sanna, "Defensive Pessimism, Optimism, and Simulating Alternatives: Some Ups and Downs of Prefactual and Counterfactual Thinking," *Journal of Personality and Social Psychology* 71 (1996): 1020–36; David R. Mandel, Denis J. Hilton, and Patrizia Catellani, *The Psychology of Counterfactual Thinking* (London: Routledge, 2005).

For counterfactuals applied to the span of Western history, see Philip E. Tetlock, Richard Ned Lebow, and Geoffrey Parker, *Unmaking the West: "What-If" Experiments That Remake World History* (Ann Arbor: University of Michigan Press, 2006). For their application to twentieth-century history and international relations, see Richard Ned Lebow, *Forbidden Fruit: Counterfactuals and International Relations* (Princeton, NJ: Princeton University Press, 2010).

CHAPTER 2

The literature on the origins of World War I is vast and in multiple languages. The best general treatments in English are Richard F. Hamilton and Holger H. Herwig, *Decision for War, 1914–1917* (New York: Cambridge University Press, 2004); Holger Afflerbach and David Stevenson, eds., *An Improbable War: The Outbreak of World War I and European Political Culture Before 1914* (New York: Berghahn Books, 2007). Both books make use of up-to-date archival information and are multicountry in focus. For excellent work on Austria and Germany see Samuel R. Williamson, *Austria-Hungary and the Origins of the First World War* (New York: St. Martin's, 1991); Annika Mombauer, *Helmuth von Moltke and the Origins of the First World War* (New York: Cambridge University Press, 2001); Annika Mombauer and Wilhelm Deist, eds., *The Kaiser: New Research on Wilhelm II's Role in Imperial Germany* (Cambridge: Cambridge University Press, 2003); Richard Ned Lebow, *A Cultural Theory of International Relations* (Cambridge: Cambridge University Press, 2008), chap. 7. For the conduct and consequences of World War I, see Hew Strachan, *The First World War* (Oxford: Oxford University Press, 2001); Holger Herwig, *The First World War: Germany and Austria-Hungary, 1914–1918* (New York: St. Martin's, 1997); David Stevenson, *Cataclysm: The First World War as Political Tragedy* (New York: Basic Books, 2005).

CHAPTER 3

This chapter draws on the same World War I literature as Chapter 2 for its analysis. For an earlier but more thoroughly documented presentation of this argument, see Chapter 3 of Lebow, *Forbidden Fruit*. The German constitutional crisis that I invent is a variant of the 1913 Zabern affair, and the best book on it remains David Schoenbaum, *Zabern 1913: Consensus Politics in Imperial Germany* (London: Allen & Unwin, 1982). Almost all the rest of the chapter I invent, although I play off many historical political, economic, scientific, and cultural developments. My argument about the decline of war draws on my own empirical study: Richard Ned Lebow, *Why Nations Fight* (Cambridge: Cambridge University Press, 2011), which is optimistic, viewing war as an obsolete and a declining institution. Had World War I been averted, the conditions associated with this decline would have become more evident earlier in the century.

The dark side of the better world stresses the intolerance of the United States and lack of civil rights for African Americans. In this connection James Gregory, *The Southern Diaspora: How the Great Migrations of Black and White Southerners Transformed America* (Chapel Hill: University of North Carolina Press, 2005), is an excellent read and the basis of my arguments in the counterfactual about what black life and opportunities would have been like in the absence of this migration. The catalyst for it was the two world wars.

CHAPTERS 4 AND 6

In these chapters I invent counterfactual lives for real and imaginary people. My starting point is always something historical. Richard Nixon, for example, was accepted by Harvard but had to decline for financial reasons. Readers interested in any of the lives of the historical figures I treat will nearly always find multiple biographies of them.

CHAPTER 5

My worse world narrative offers a different outcome to the invented German constitutional crisis and speculates about its implications for the political development of Germany and Europe. It makes use of the same sources as Chapters 3 and 4.

The limited nuclear exchange assumes the difficulty of controlling alerted nuclear forces, a phenomenon well documented during the Cold War. For relevant literature here see Paul Bracken, *The Command and Control of Nuclear Forces* (New Haven, CT: Yale University Press, 1983), 56; Richard Ned Lebow, *Nuclear Crisis Management: A Dangerous Illusion* (Ithaca, NY: Cornell University Press, 1987).

CHAPTER 7

This chapter reflects on the arguments of the book. The only new empirical material concerns non-European countries, most notably China. There is currently a great debate about China's foreign policy goals. Worthwhile reading includes Peter Hays Gries, *China's New Nationalism: Pride, Politics, and Diplomacy* (Berkeley: University of California Press, 2004); Alastair Ian Johnston and Robert S. Ross, eds., *New Directions in the Study of China's Foreign Policy* (Stanford, CA: Stanford University Press, 2006); David M. Lampton, *The Three Faces of Chinese Power: Might, Money, and Minds* (Berkeley: University of California Press, 2008); Robert S. Ross and Zhe Feng, *China's Ascent: Power, Security, and the Future of International Politics* (Ithaca, NY: Cornell University Press, 2008).

Index